The Foundations of Research

Jonathan Grix

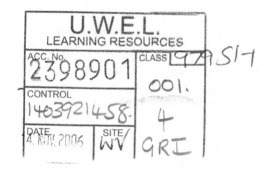

palgrave
macmillan

First published 2004 by
PALGRAVE MACMILLAN
Houndmills, Basingstoke, Hampshire RG21 6XS and
175 Fifth Avenue, New York, N.Y. 10010
Companies and representatives throughout the world

PALGRAVE MACMILLAN is the global academic imprint of the Palgrave
Macmillan division of St. Martin's Press, LLC and of Palgrave Macmillan Ltd.
Macmillan® is a registered trademark in the United States, United Kingdom
and other countries. Palgrave is a registered trademark in the European
Union and other countries.

ISBN-13: 978–1–4039–2145–1 paperback
ISBN-10: 1–4039–2145–8 paperback

This book is printed on paper suitable for recycling and made from fully
managed and sustained forest sources.

A catalogue record for this book is available from the British Library.

A catalog record for this book is available from the Library of Congress.
Library of Congress Catalog Code Number: 2004050423

10   9   8   7   6   5   4   3   2
13 12 11 10 09 08 07 06 05

Printed in China

for Kevin

Contents

List of Figures

List of Tables

Preface

Many of the ideas in this book have developed during the teaching of the 'Introduction to social research' course in the School of Social Sciences at the University of Birmingham. This course, in turn, was originally based around a previous book, *Demystifying Postgraduate Research*. The origins of that book stemmed from a pub discussion with Charlie Jeffery and the idea of developing a course designed to describe the nuts and bolts of research to fledgling postgraduates at the Institute for German Studies.

The present book carries forward and builds upon the rationale for all of the above: the need for students and scholars to understand the tools and terminology of research before they begin actual research. Advanced undergraduates, postgraduates and researchers all need to familarise themselves with the language of research, in order to understand and to produce clear academic work themselves. It is to these groups that this book is addressed. For first-time researchers (undertaking an undergraduate or Master's dissertation) the book offers a guide to the basic scaffolding of research tools and terms; for the doctoral student and researcher, it provides a reference for particular areas of a study (for example, ontological and epistemological issues), and for all groups it functions as an accompaniment to courses in research methods and methodology.

The list of people who helped shape the circumstances in which this book was written and who contributed directly with ideas and suggestions is long. First and foremost, I would like to thank Willie Paterson for providing the environment in which to think about such a project and the encouragement to pursue it in the first place. I have been fortunate enough to enjoy Willie's support for this undertaking and, more widely, in academic life in general. Colin Hay was kind enough to look through and comment on two chapters for me. Apart from his wide knowledge of methodological issues, Colin has the ability to make me laugh out loud with his insightful criticisms. Thanks, also, to Dave Marsh for helpful discussions and ideas. I would also like to thank Steve Davies, Anna Brown (historians) and Roger E. Backhouse (economist) who offered advice on sections of Chapter 5 (they also warned me against the oversimplifications that I have made). I have also benefited from Andrew Thompson's comments on surveys, and, on the 'Introduction to social research' module, from discussions with students, who, coming from a wide variety of backgrounds, have asked the kind of questions I seek to answer in this book.

Alec McAulay, whose chaotic working style produced some excellent results at the University of Birmingham Press, kindly allowed me to make use of material previously published in *Demystifying Postgraduate Research*.

Many thanks for the useful and encouraging comments of two anonymous reviewers, whose suggestions have helped shape the volume.

Finally, thanks to Louis and Hannah for keeping me sane and Andrea, my wife, for her constant support. I had never believed in serendipity until my long-time friend, Kevin, needed someone to accompany him on a trip to Berlin after another friend had dropped out. As a result of my last-minute decision to go to Berlin, I met Andrea and the rest is history. For this reason I dedicate this book to Kevin. Thanks, mate.

Introduction

The purpose of this volume is to introduce and discuss the foundations of research. The main aim is to equip students with some of the most important tools and terminology of research as well as with an understanding of these terms. If you command the basic vocabulary of generic research, you are far more likely to choose the correct theories, concepts or methods to use in your work. By grasping the core tools used in research, much of the mystery that can surround it begins to disappear.

Moreover, knowledge of the 'nuts and bolts' that make up social research can go a long way to ensuring that the tools of research are used properly. If you have the right equipment and you know how to employ it, the research process becomes a great deal easier and quicker. In the following chapters, then, I am interested in clarifying the terms and terminology associated with research – that is, any research, whatever discipline within the human sciences – and to offer an introductory, and, hopefully, thought-provoking discussion on some of the key issues in research. The text is thus generic and non-disciplinary; that is, it takes a step back from disciplines and their assumptions and presents the tools common to most social research.

My target audience is advanced undergraduates and those undertaking postgraduate taught and research degrees. I am primarily interested in the social sciences and those parts of the humanities, especially history, that deal with social phenomena. Instead of repeating that mouthful throughout the book, I shall opt for the shorthand 'human sciences' whenever I wish to refer to the area this volume is intended to cover. The issues dealt with in this book, though, are important for a wide range of academic disciplines and not, as is mistakenly believed, just for political scientists and sociologists. *All* students and scholars in the human sciences – this ranges from cultural studies, through history and economics to social psychology and international relations – need to know, be clear about and reflect upon the foundations of research.

The following chapters are not only about defining the key terminology of the foundations of research, but they also address some of the most fundamental issues concerning research in the human sciences. These include the so-called 'dichotomies' of quantitative vs. qualitative research strategies, the structure–agency problem and inductive vs. deductive research strategies. As will become apparent, I believe that these dichotomies have their use in discerning between specific aspects in research, but I also believe they should be seen as complementary and not opposing entities. A few quick examples will suffice at this stage.

Given the temporal constraints of most research, and the fact that a researcher needs some sort of guide to her pursuit of knowledge, *some form of preconceived idea, notion or hunch* is essential to begin the research process (this is the basis of the 'induction–deduction' dichotomy, see chapter 6). Indeed, without it there is nothing to animate a research question or design, or to motivate research in the first place. Even strong supporters of research that generates theory will have gone into the field with some preconceived ideas of what they were looking for. Equally, as will become apparent, the 'quantitative–qualitative' divide among researchers, who disagree about the role of theory in research and, above all, about 'the sequence and relationship of activities involved' (Robson 1995: 18) in the process, is rarely reflected in real-life research projects (see chapter 7).

Throughout the following chapters, I take you through the most important foundations of the research process and clarify many of the concepts used in the human sciences. I approach the process of uncovering the foundations of research from a *generic* angle, rather than from any specific discipline within the human sciences. The building blocks of research are similar for all disciplines with this focus. It is the order and level of importance given to the core components of research, and the philosophical assumptions that underlie them, that distinguishes one discipline's methodological approach from another.

Finally, the book is designed to be both a reference text as well as a logically constructed book, with chapters building on previous chapters. There is a full glossary in the appendix which can be referred to and an index to locate areas of interest. Indeed, it may be a good first step to look through the glossary to familiarise yourself with some of the terms and ideas there.

▶ The structure of the book

The book is divided into nine chapters. **Chapter 1** introduces the nature of research. First, I touch on the language used in research and why it is necessary to understand it. Then I turn to the nature of and difference between BA/BSc, MA and PhD research, allowing a little extra space for the latter, as the PhD does differ from a first degree and MA in many ways. The rest of the chapter offers advice on thinking about where to study, as it is very important to find a good match between what you want to study and the facilities and resources of the place where you wish to study. Further, I discuss how to manage your time, a crucial element of any successful research strategy and the need to familiarise yourself with and prepare yourself for the task ahead. It is surprising how many students launch themselves into their dissertation or thesis without being fully aware of what is expected of them.

An introduction to, and discussion of, the all-important tools and terminology which make up the 'nuts and bolts' of research, and by which research is conducted, is the main subject of the second section in **chapter 2**. The aim is to demystify the terminology and to reveal the core theoretical and analytical questions that must be addressed in any piece of research. As I have already suggested, it is only with a clear understanding of the terminology employed in research and the underlying issues this terminology reflects that you can begin planning your project. You are advised to reflect not only on the variety of meanings of a specific concept, but on its origins. Chapter 2 also briefly discusses and clarifies key concepts and terms, such as typologies, ideal types, paradigms, methods and methodology. The important concept of 'theory' is dealt with at length in a separate chapter (6). The idea here, as elsewhere in this text, is not to replace a comprehensive course in research methods, but rather to put you in a position to understand and even enjoy a methods course and to be more reflexive in your own studies. You will also be in a position to identify the essential parts of the research process most relevant to your project.

This prepares the way for **chapter 3**, 'Getting Started in Research', which turns its attention to the mechanics of research and the foundations of the research process. As focusing your topic early is very important, this chapter concentrates on:

- developing research questions or hypotheses with which to guide your research
- the process of defining and refining a research question or hypothesis
- the relationship between the research question or hypothesis and the methods and sources to be employed in your work.

The necessity of arriving at a set of research questions or hypotheses cannot be overstated, for without specific questions you will not be able to organise your project. This is not to imply that research questions cannot be generated from fieldwork (the inductive method). However, on a pragmatic level, few students have the time or funds to gather sufficient quantities of data with the intention of finding relevant questions or observing specific phenomena, especially given the limited time they have to finish their projects.

Chapter 3 also introduces the notion of a continuum of literature reviews, ranging from the most common starting point of research (i.e. familiarising yourself with a topic) to speed reading texts after fieldwork and data analysis. The latter sections of the chapter are given over to a brief discussion of the level of analysis you choose in your project. This leads on to one of the most important themes in the human sciences, the structure and agency problem. After a summary of what is usually understood under these two concepts, I outline the two most common 'types' of research that are on offer: case-study and comparative.

Chapter 4 offers a discussion of the building blocks in the foundations of research: ontology and epistemology. A lot of mystery surrounds these concepts and it is my intention to present you with an accessible introduction to understanding *what* these concepts mean, *why* they are essential to our research and *how* they relate to other key building blocks of research. This I do by presenting the thesis of a directional relationship between ontology, epistemology, methodology, methods and even sources. The purpose of this complicated-sounding exercise is quite simple: to show how a person's starting point in research (their ontological position) has major implication for a) what they believe we can and should research and b) how we can go about researching it. By doing so, this chapter brings to light the influence traditions of research have on the entire research process. By bringing clarity to the foundations of research, we place ourselves in a position of knowledge, one from which it is possible to adjudicate between the myriad of approaches to social phenomena on offer. Without such clarity and knowledge of the basics, we run the risk of simply arguing past each other.

Chapter 5 builds on chapter 4 by offering an overview of the key traditions in social research and examples of the main perspectives in economics, political science, international relations, sociology and historical studies respectively. Although there are a great number of books dealing with the key research paradigms on the market, many of which go into minute detail, I think it a good idea to present at least the contours of the key traditions of positivism, (critical) realism and interpretivism. Additionally, I shall briefly introduce post-modernism and feminism, which do not share the long history of the other conventional traditions, but nonetheless need to be discussed, as the challenges they pose to research thinking are to be taken seriously.

The second section of chapter 5 offers a brief description of the disciplinary perspectives that fall under the broad umbrella of 'positivism' by presenting their aims, key assumptions, key themes, key concepts, limitations, chief advocates and seminal works. Such a wide overview will arm you further with most of the terms and terminology you are likely to encounter in your studies, thereby exposing you to the language of research. In addition, and of equal importance, I shall align these perspectives according to their research paradigm (positivism, inter-pretivism, etc.), in order to show the similarities/dissimilarities among certain perspectives. Although this method of grouping and categorising academic perspectives may be seen as crude – given that it is difficult, and not necessarily desirable, to shoehorn perspectives into certain categories – it nonetheless offers an overview of an often impenetrable and overwhelming area of study. It will also, I hope, encourage you to think beyond narrow disciplinary boundaries.

There is perhaps no more confusing concept in research than that of theory. For this reason **chapter 6** is given over to discussing theory and its role in research. Unlike many of the concepts introduced in chapter 2, 'theory' is unable to be fixed in meaning and thus avoids a simple, single definition. What we can do, however, is discuss in detail why it has come to mean what it has – a 'testable' proposition, a hypo-thetical statement against which 'reality' is tested in the field – with reference to the influence of positivism and positivist research. Once we understand that this is simply *one* way of conceiving of theory, we are ready to discuss others. This is done with reference to the traditions of research above, and how they conceive of theory, and to the many different types of theory available in research.

Chapter 7 is built around the 'quantitative–qualitative' dichotomy. Here I discuss some examples of methods commonly used to collect and analyse empirical data, including interviews, participant observation, documentary analysis and media analysis. The purpose of the methods section is not to offer a comprehensive account of types of procedures for data collection and analysis, but rather to introduce a series of empirical methods and to indicate how the choice of which ones to use in a study is governed by a certain *logic* contained in the methodology employed or the rationale of the research.

In addition to an overview of some of the most frequently used methods in the human sciences, I turn my attention to the notion of 'mixing methods' and 'triangulation of methods' in research. Both of these notions are not without problems and need to be thought about carefully.

Chapter 8 highlights two important aspects of research for students to be aware of: the danger of accidental plagiarism by improper referencing and poor note-taking, and the sensitive topic of ethics. Whilst ethics has always been important in research, plagiarism has become increasingly so, especially as the Internet now offers an unquantifiable amount of easily accessible information to download. In this section I also discuss what constitutes proper referencing and how to avoid being accused of cheating.

Ethics play a major part in any empirical research undertaken, especially when involving people. After an initial discussion of the roots of ethics in social research, I give examples for you to think through. I also present a continuum along which I place certain types of research: for example, covert undercover reporting, 'borrowing' documents, interviews and 'deception' research (i.e. dressing up and posing as a policeman). At this point we are close to the nitty-gritty of research: your awareness of professional academic standards and how they impinge upon your research project.

Finally, **chapter 9** contains the conclusion, which sums up the important messages that I hope you will take away from reading this book.

Appendix 1 offers you a discussion on the possible sequencing of research stages, an idea that simplifies and facilitates the research process. Here I set out a guideline to the process of research that can be adapted and adjusted to suit individual needs and circumstances. As I shall show, it is important for students to *imagine* the direction their research will take at a very early stage. Breaking the research process up into manageable and comprehensible stages is all part of a successful research strategy, so long as you retain a sense of the whole project. Students will see that there is an inherent logic, albeit not always the same in each case, to the research process and that the stages presented impact greatly on one another and are interlinked.

Appendix 2, on the other hand, consists of a glossary of some of the key terms used and often misunderstood in research. All of the terms in **bold** in the main text can be found in the glossary. The glossary can be used as a reference guide while reading this and other texts, but will remain a useful companion throughout the course of research. The choice of terms has been driven by their importance for research in the human sciences, with a focus on the building blocks essential to most research. Finally, I offer some examples of proper referencing techniques most commonly used in the human sciences.

Throughout the book my emphasis, then, is on clarity and practicality, on how understanding the foundations of research leads to better and clearer research.

1 The Nature of Research

> *Chapter 1 introduces:*
>
> - *The 'language' of research*
> - *The nature of research*
> - *The idea of preparing yourself by considering where to study, time management and by familiarising yourself with the task ahead*

The aim of this first chapter is to begin to familiarise you with the nature, tools and terminology of the research process. Central to my aims is the 'demystification' of research, be it a BSc or BA dissertation, an MSc, MA, MPhil, PhD or DPhil. The emphasis is on the *foundations of research* and many of the terms and much of the process will be applicable to all sustained research in the human sciences. The following advice will also be of interest to researchers who have to write lengthy dissertations or structured research reports. From time to time it will be necessary to address specific points relating to a higher degree, i.e. the PhD, as these are not relevant to advanced undergraduates or all postgraduate work. The majority of the points made, however, are fundamental to all research. This chapter also touches on the differences between undergraduate, postgraduate and especially PhD research.

First, I discuss the language of research; that is, the manner in which it is presented and why it is important to learn the generic terms of research in order to dispel the mystery surrounding the -isms and -ologies that pepper research papers, research methods books and courses. I then turn to the nature of research, distinguishing between under-graduate dissertations, MAs and PhDs. Phds get a special section, because they differ in so many ways to the former two. The final three sections touch on where to study, time management and familiarising yourself with the task ahead. All of these factors are relevant for what I am concerned with here: the foundations of research. The choice of where to study is most relevant for postgraduates, but also for those undergraduates wishing to continue their studies. Time management is essential for both undergraduates and postgraduates. Finally, we turn to the most obvious, yet underused idea of simply looking at what it is you are supposed to be producing. Before we can embellish our work with wonderful, sophisticated and insightful statements, we need to know the mechanics of research: what does a dissertation or thesis look like?

▶ The 'language' of research

Whilst we all know the old cliché, 'knowledge is power', it is worth reflecting on the ways in which knowledge is discussed, disputed and disseminated. In the human sciences there are a number of different 'discourses' between disciplines, for example economics, history and cultural studies. Common to most discourses is the basic language of research. Given the variety of uses of the terms and terminology of human science research, it is hardly surprising that students rarely have a firm grasp of the tools of their trade. Different academics in different disciplines attach a wide range of meanings and interpretations to the terminology of research. One person's 'theory' is another's 'taxonomy', while another researcher's 'ideal type' is another's 'theory', and so on. With little or no knowledge of the standard reference points in general research, you are likely to produce a dissertation or thesis which is unclear and imprecise; learning the rules of the game simplifies the process, makes it transparent and takes away the fear associated with the unknown. It is my contention that in order to be able to work within the parameters of the human sciences, you need to be very clear about what the tools and terminology of research are and what they mean *before* you can begin researching. If you spend a little time learning the language of research, learning what the terms and concepts mean and how they can be employed, the mystery associated with much of academic work, especially at the postgraduate level, will begin to disappear.

This may sound trivial, but given the fact that many students – and seasoned academics for that matter – have difficulty in differentiating between crucial terms such as ontology (what is out there to know about) and epistemology (what and how can we know about it), their subsequent research is bound to suffer, as knowledge of these two key terms and their place in research is essential to understanding the research process as a whole.

These particular terms (ontology and epistemology) are often shrouded in ambiguity, partly created by the language in which they are explained, leaving the reader more confused than she was before she began reading. There is an obvious and urgent need for agreement on the meaning of specific generic terms across the disciplines in the human sciences to prevent the confusion which surrounds many concepts at present. Suffice it to say that this should not be understood as a call for unity of methodological approaches, as diversity is essential for the vibrancy of the human sciences, but rather a call for clarity on key terms that can travel across disciplines.

What other reasons are there for needing to know and understand standard terms and concepts in social research? A simple example will do: consider a would-be bricklayer who does not know the difference between a trowel, a spirit level and a chisel. These are the basic tools of his trade, without which no wall can be built. Each tool has a specific purpose and, if it were used wrongly (or in the wrong order), for example taking a chisel to lay bricks, the results would be disastrous. In research, specific tools have specific purposes and, if one is to employ them correctly, one must first understand what they mean, what they are meant to do and how and when to use them. The lack of clarity and constancy of the social-research lexicon has led to a minefield of misused, abused and misunderstood terms and phrases with which students must contend. It has also led to confusion surrounding the presentation of assumptions upon which research is based. There is a need to be clear about these assumptions and a need to know the research traditions from which these assumptions spring. Thus, by familiarising ourselves with the technical language of research, we effectively demystify it.

No discussion about the language of research can, however, avoid mentioning the bewildering array of -isms and -ologies used in presenting research. Many of these terms are used wrongly or imprecisely, which adds to the mystery of research and the impenetrability of much of its output. Use of specific terms, for example 'variables', 'relationships', 'measuring', 'co-variation' and 'hypotheses' (see also Ragin 1994: 11–13), denote a sense of seriousness, of sound academic judgement, but the fact of the matter is that merely using specific terms is no guarantee of solid research. Many researchers, as we shall see in the following chapters, refuse to use such a language when undertaking and presenting their work, as they seek to distance themselves from particular research paradigms (most notably 'positivism' – see chapter 5).

▶ The nature of research

Undergraduate dissertations and MA dissertations have many things in common. Both are pieces of sustained research of up to and around 10 000–15 000 words. It is often said that the best undergraduate essay gets near to or attains Master's level of work. At the Master's level, students are expected to be far more independent in their choice and execution of research projects. Also, a Master's would usually contain an empirical case-study, unless, of course, its key concern was of a more theoretical nature. Such an empirical study usually means a sustained amount of time spent on fieldwork, something only a minority of undergraduates would have the time or resources to do. Nonetheless, a solid undergraduate dissertation should exhibit some characteristics similar to those of an MA dissertation: a clear presentation of the problem; clear research questions or hypotheses; a discussion of the methods, methodology and sources employed in the project; a section which attempts to address the research questions posed, and a clear evaluation of the findings. Each of these sections, as I shall point out throughout the following chapters, is logically interlinked.

If we leave the differences to one side, the question still remains: what is research? Generally speaking, research at BA, MA and PhD level will have a number of things in common:

1 You will have a question to ask or problem to solve (chapter 3 discusses how to arrive at such a question).
2 You will set about answering your question by sifting through a variety of data and sources, using specific research methods (chapter 7 introduces the most well-known).
3 You will need a methodology to be able to answer your questions (chapters 2, 3, 4 and 5 discuss the underpinnings of research).
4 You will need to think about how your project adds to knowledge on this topic either by generating new knowledge or clarifying or furthering existing work.

The distance between a solid MA (Master of Arts; *Magister Artium*) dissertation and a PhD is less great than that between BA (Bachelor of Arts; *Baccalaureus Artium*) and PhD (Doctor of Philosophy; *Philosophea Doctor*), as the Master's student will already have had to contend with many issues confronting a doctoral candidate. The leap from a BA to a PhD is great, but not unbridgeable. The most obvious unique aspect of **doctoral research** is the emphasis it places on the individual. There are few taught elements of the degree, except for research training, and the student is expected to have a high level of self-discipline in order to be able to cope with only minimal guidance and structure – in comparison to what students at BA or MA level are used to. (This is not the case in the USA, where PhDs entail required coursework.) In addition, PhD students will have to go through a comprehensive **viva** examination, defending the work they have submitted. Self-discipline, of course, is needed for all types of sustained research and is easier to produce if you have a keen interest in a subject in the first place. This makes the choice of topic important for undergraduates, essential for an MA and absolutely crucial for a PhD.

▶ The nature of the doctoral process

A PhD can be successfully completed by anyone who has a certain amount of intelligence, and, importantly, the degree of commitment necessary. This is not to suggest that obtaining a doctorate is easy. Commitment and steely determination are essential, but of little use if not accompanied by an open and enquiring mind and a willingness to take criticism and advice and to listen and learn from others. Herein lies the first difficulty: to complete a higher degree successfully, you will have to reassess and recalibrate your often deeply-held opinions in the light of the new material, arguments and debates that you will encounter on your learning journey.

The first thing to note about a PhD is what it is not. It is rarely a magnum opus, the study of all studies ever on a specific topic (many educational systems, for example Germany, cater for this by offering a higher doctorate option). There is plenty of time to produce this after-wards, as most great thinkers in fact have. For example, Albert Einstein and Karl Marx made relatively modest contributions to their fields of research in their doctoral theses, but they spent that time learning the tools of their trade whilst 'demonstrating their fully professional mastery of the established paradigms' in their field (Phillips and Pugh 1994: 35).

Undertaking a PhD should be seen as a learning process, an apprenticeship in the art of research in which you will learn to reflect on the origins of theories and concepts, how to theorise, how to mesh theory with practice, and how to prioritise and organise a vast quantity of material into a readable text within a restricted period of time. The discipline necessary for successfully completing a doctorate will benefit the student far beyond the walls of academia. There is no doubt that a solid formal education will help you undertake a doctorate, but other factors such as mental agility, inquisitiveness, motivation and discipline, which can be acquired outside the school gates, are also beneficial.

▶ Why do a PhD?

Denis Lawton makes a valid point in stating that just because you are interested in something does not necessarily mean you should write a PhD on it. You may be better off producing another kind of book, one without the constraints and 'hoops' a PhD candidate is required to jump through (Lawton 1999: 3). However, the combination of both your interest and ability should ensure that you have a good chance of being successful over the sustained period of study. The point here is not to do a doctorate for the sake of it. The title 'Dr' may be elevating – for a short while – but that is not a good enough reason for spending at least three years studying hard. As a researcher, you should be aiming to contribute something new to an existing body of knowledge and, if you cannot, you do not have a PhD thesis.

What you should avoid in all cases is to end up simply adding to the increasing mountain of monographs, a scenario in which, as George Steiner puts it, 'the true source of Z's tome is X's and Y's work on the identical subject' (Steiner 1991: 39). Instead, what you should aim to do is to come as close as possible to what Steiner terms 'the immediate', or, in the manner in which I interpret it here, the event you are attempting to shed light on or explain. The point of research should not be to give an analysis of a critique of an event, but to deliver an interpretation of the event itself. You need the tertiary material (texts on texts) and the secondary material (others' work on the event) to position and guide your work and to situate your contribution, but the aim is to complement this with primary or new material, or with a novel interpretation. There is a certain tension here with the need to produce original work within a restricted period of time.

▶ The right place to study

If you are finishing a first degree and wish to continue with your studies, now is the time to consider the right place for you and your project, as choosing the right department in the first instance is crucial. If you wish to undertake a taught Master's, you need to think very carefully about the 'fit' between what's on offer and where you want to go. If you are taking a doctorate, you need to consider a number of factors: if there are only two other postgraduates in a given department, one working on a Marxist interpretation of Franz Kafka's *Das Schloss* and the other on an econometric analysis of Dollar–Deutschmark exchange-rate dynamics, you are not going into the best environment for, say, studying the impact of the Iraq war on European–US relations. Apart from the fact that this department will probably not have a European or US expert, you will be isolated in your studies, with little chance of either the type of feedback you require or the opportunities to present ongoing work in postgraduate seminars.

Do not let your choice of department be guided solely by an internationally renowned scholar – if there are half a dozen in the department, then that is fine. Otherwise, leading scholars have a tendency to be in great demand and will almost certainly have a large number of Master's and doctoral students, a heavy conference schedule (i.e. they are very often abroad when you need to see them) and may be hard to make an appointment with. Their turnaround time on giving feedback on versions of your work – an important part of your development – could be months. If, however, there are a number of capable scholars in a given department, this will be less of a concern, as you will always have somebody with whom you can discuss your ideas, providing your topic chimes with the research interests of the department. Remember, too, the dangers associated with all supervisors, celebrities or not. These include:

- you doing your supervisor's project
- you never being able to come up with an original idea (because he or she has been there, done that, etc.)
- a general lack of confidence in your own judgements and an over-reliance on the supervisor and, especially, his or her knowledge of the subject.

Whatever postgraduate degree you do, you do need, however, someone who knows what an MA, MPhil or PhD consists of and who is at least halfway *interested* in your subject area and is sensitive to how *you* want to approach it. For research degrees you should, ideally, seek joint supervision (see Wisker 2001: 22–8 for a further discussion on 'where to study' and for differences between degrees).

▶ Matters of time

Good time-management skills are of paramount importance in research, and now is the moment to give these some thought. A major problem for undergraduates contemplating their extended essay is all the other work and assignments they need to submit beforehand. Even so, you need to give some thought to your dissertation a long time in advance of starting it. One of the main reasons for this is that gathering information and data for an extended essay takes far more time than writing it up.

A slow start will inevitably translate into a mad rush towards the end of the period of study. Try not to get into the habit of burning the midnight oil and waking up at two o'clock in the afternoon. A good night's sleep and a regular work pattern will probably lead to better results in the end. Remember also to leave time for life outside your studies, as merely immersing yourself in your studies without coming up for air could lead to a number of problems. First, you need time off from direct studying, so that you can recover, absorb and reflect on everything you have been thinking, reading and writing about. Secondly, if you give up previous hobbies or socialising to fit in a few hours of extra reading, the results may be counter-productive. You need to feel 'balanced' within yourself, a state that will obviously differ from person to person (see May 1999: 62–3). This is, after all, what you will hopefully aspire to post-degree, so you may as well start now.

Reasons for bad time management are manifold: for example, the perfectionist who refuses to write but continues to gather data will eventually be buried under a pile of information with little or nothing to show for it. The perfectionist would also not have had the benefit of frequent exchanges with her dissertation tutor or supervisor and thus run the risk of 'going off at a tangent', that is, digressing from her area of enquiry. Perfectionism may be a virtue to some, but under conditions of tight time constraints, it could prevent a person from actually achieving anything. Other reasons for delays include distraction from the task in hand. This can come in many forms, including having to work to make ends meet – a particular concern for many part-time students holding down a job. Once the research momentum is broken, it is very difficult to find your way back in.

Postgraduate studies in particular demand constant application and concentration for a longer period of time, and students ought to ask themselves whether they are willing to enter into this commitment before beginning their studies. On the positive side, research is a gradual process of accumulating knowledge, which brings with it a sense of achievement and confidence that, in turn, makes the whole process more enjoyable and may lead to publication or conference papers en route.

▶ Familiarise yourself

Fear of the unknown, the esoteric and the complex only hinders progress. By seeing the research process stripped bare, revealing the factors that constitute good scholarship, you will be in a position to overcome these fears.

There are a number of things that will make the research process far more productive and enjoyable and allow you to 'hit the ground running'. These range from learning to assess the manageability of your project, to getting to know what it is that constitutes an undergraduate dissertation, MA, MPhil or PhD in the first place. Taking some time at the beginning of your studies to familiarise yourself with what lies before you will save time in the long run: the 'hares' who throw themselves into writing their dissertations or theses with little consideration for university regulations, the format or the word length are often overtaken by the 'tortoises' who allowed themselves sufficient time to study the research terrain before beginning.

Surprisingly, many students do not have a clue what their **dissertation** or **thesis** is supposed to consist of beyond the word-limit and, perhaps, the intimidatory sentence in university handbooks (for PhDs) calling for 'works that contribute substantially to human knowledge'. This sentence is enough to put off the brightest student. The point here is that if you do not know what constitutes the degree you are aiming for, you are not going to be able to map out a plan of how to get there. Imagine training for a race and not knowing the distance to be run. It is no good being a good sprinter if the race turns out to be over ten miles. Hence, you will need to familiarise yourself with what is expected of you *before* you begin. By looking at past dissertations or theses of previous students from your department – they are usually all collected in the departments themselves or the main university library – you can learn several things. What is the average length? What is the ratio of empirical material to the literature review and theoretical approach in your particular department and topic area? Familiarise yourself with the structure of the theses and, after a while, a pattern may emerge. Here is a standard example which will assist in highlighting specific components of research (however, bear in mind that this is only one model of research and it should *not be considered as fixed*):

1 introduction
2 literature review
3 methodology
4 case-study(ies)/empirical section
5 evaluation
6 conclusion
7 appendices and bibliography.

This example is certainly valid for many standard social-science dissertations and theses. In the humanities, however, the stages high-lighted above may be less pronounced. You will, however, have a begin-ning and an end. You must also connect your work with a wider literature (no. 2 above) and your project will exhibit, perhaps implicitly, a methodology (no. 3) and a case-study or subject (no. 4). You will also have to evaluate and sum up your work. The difference is that, in the social sciences, the above sections are more likely to be clearly distin-guishable from one another. The simple advice here is that you should acquaint yourself with the task ahead. By having a rough idea of what you are aiming at, you manage to dispel many myths and anxieties and you can already begin to have a mental picture of the logic of research. By breaking down your project into broad parts, as in the example above, you can begin to get a feel of what it comprises.

Once you have familiarised yourself with dissertations and theses in your department and university, the best advice is to consider the format and presentation of your own work in this light. Usually, the university library or your department will have a pamphlet on how to present your work, including page set-up (size of margins), font size, how to use footnotes and references and word-length (check whether this includes or excludes appendices, tables, diagrams, bibliography and footnotes). Look at this before you start any writing, for if you set up your project and your computer in the format and style (point size, paragraph, page set-up, etc.) stipulated in your department's or university's regulations, you can use this for all subsequent work on your project and you will save yourself no end of trouble when you come to put together its con-stituent parts. Setting out the format early does not, however, mean that the first sections or ideas you put down on paper are fixed. On the contrary, you will need to go over and redraft sections and chapters several times before they are actually finished.

Summary

The opening chapter offers you some rudimentary advice on what to think about prior to commencing your studies. In particular I have highlighted the following:

- The nature of, and difference between, an undergraduate dissertation, Master's and doctorate.
- The need to learn the specific 'language' of research and why this is important at this early stage.
- The need to reflect on the type of degree you wish to undertake.
- The need to consider carefully, as far as it is possible given financial constraints, the place where you choose to study.
- The need to develop a regular working pattern to achieve the best results.
- The need to find out exactly what it is you are supposed to do by familiarising yourself as soon as possible with dissertations and theses at your chosen institution (look up previous examples of your degree).

▶ Further reading

Burnham, P. (ed.) (1997) *Surviving the Research Process in Politics*, London and Washington, DC, Pinter.

Graves, N. and Varma, V. (eds) (1999) *Working for a Doctorate. A Guide for the Humanities and Social Sciences*, London and New York, Routledge, especially chapters 1, 4 and 10.

Phillips, E.M. and Pugh, D.S. (eds) (1994) *How to Get a PhD: A Handbook for Students and Their Supervisors*, Buckingham and Philadelphia, PA, Open University Press, chapters 1–4.

Wisker, G. (2001) *The Postgraduate Handbook. Succeed with your MA, MPhil, EdD and PhD*, Basingstoke, Palgrave Macmillan, chapter 1.

2 The 'Nuts and Bolts' of Research

> Chapter 2 introduces:
>
> - *The key tools used in research: theory, model, typology, ideal type, paradigm, concept and the abuse of concepts*
> - *The key terms used in research: methods and methodology*

In this chapter I set out to 'demystify' the research process by introducing and explaining the generic meanings of the key tools and terms used in research across the human sciences. Naturally, I have been very selective in the choice of tools and terms included; however, most students will come across them in their studies. You should look upon them as the 'scaffolding' around which the language of research is built. Now, this may strike you as an exercise akin to watching paint dry, yet, as I highlighted in the previous chapter, if you learn the 'language' of research, you are far more likely to produce a clear and precise piece of work. The tools and terms discussed in this chapter are often understood wrongly, used indiscriminately and employed interchangeably. The result is confusion within disciplines and a lack of dialogue between disciplines.

▶ The tools of research

It is my contention that while *discipline-specific* terms and concepts exist and have their uses (e.g. 'supply and demand' in economics; 'policy-transfer' in political science; 'social stratification' in sociology, etc.), generic research terms and concepts *have the same fundamental meaning in whatever discipline they are used*. This holds true for all the tools I shall introduce except the concept of 'theory'. While the tools below may have a generic meaning that can travel across disciplines, 'theory' is less easy to pin down. This is due to the role theory plays in social research, a role complicated by the fact that it is utilised for different purposes by different academic perspectives, working in different philosophical traditions (see chapter 5). For this reason I shall not include a discussion of theory here, but rather in chapter 6 which is devoted entirely to understanding theory and its role in research.

A good way to introduce key concepts used in research is to suggest a continuum of research tools that have as their intention 'explaining' social phenomena at one end and 'describing' social phenomena at the other. This is, of course, an oversimplification for the purpose of understanding. Along this continuum it is possible to place the tools in question (they are: **theory**, **model**, **typology**, **ideal type**, **paradigm** and **concept**):

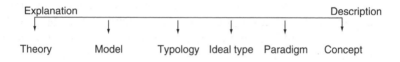

In general terms the above continuum can be understood as a range of tools employed in social research for different purposes. As with all the broad categorisations made throughout this book, the above continuum is a rough guide and not a precise description. I have listed the research tools in order of their ability to *explain* social phenomena. All of these tools can be looked upon as classificatory devices; that is, they help us make sense of, categorise, understand and explain diverse social phenomena. Theory is the most complex tool used in social research and concepts are the least complex, although this is not to suggest that some concepts or 'concept-clusters' (i.e. more than one concept constituting a phrase, for example 'conditional loyalty' – see below for more on this) cannot be made to accommodate complex issues. An 'explanation' is not to be understood as being better or more significant than a 'description' of an event. The point is that different academic disciplines have different purposes and aims: scholars undertaking historical studies in general do not employ a specific 'theory' or 'model', but would not be averse to employing a 'typology', 'ideal type' or set of 'concepts' to describe and attempt to understand particular events. Many historians and numerous other scholars in different disciplines who maintain that they simply 'get on with the job of research' and leave 'theorising' to methodologists, are, ironically, making theoretical claims about the status and nature of knowledge (on historians see Fulbrook 2002). As I shall show, *all* research is underpinned by meta-theoretical assumptions (see chapters 4 and 5 for a deeper discussion of this). On the other hand, many political scientists would want to 'explain' or even attempt to 'predict' future events or actors' behaviour by adopting and using models and theories.

The following section runs through the terms on the continuum, giving their root definitions and examples of how they are used in research.

Model, typology and ideal type

Model

A model is a representation of something, in the way that a model aeroplane is a replica of a real aeroplane. A model can be both a descriptive and an exploratory device. A road map and a wiring diagram are good examples of descriptive models (Walliman 2001: 248), with the former selecting key characteristics or features of how the land lies and the latter depicting *exactly* where the live wires are. The accuracy of a wiring diagram is a case of life and death. In social research, on the other hand, models are less accurate and this inaccuracy is rarely so dangerous. Some academics attempt to represent reality by a series of boxes and arrows which depict and attempt to make explicit significant relationships between specific aspects of the model; thus a model 'enables the formulation of empirically testable propositions regarding the nature of these relationships' (Frankfort-Nachmias and Nachmias 1992: 44). A significant number of academics in political science, and especially economics, swear by the use of modelling as a way of ensuring rigorous research. Models can help us 'predict' human actions, for example how people are likely to vote. Such assumptions about the ability of social research to 'explain' human behaviour are usually linked to the research tradition of 'positivism' and those academics operating within it (see chapter 5 for a further discussion of this and other research traditions). A number of scholars, as I shall show, share neither the assumptions made by positivists (and the language they employ) nor the modelling method used to study human behaviour. It is less important *whether* you use a model in your work, but more *what you believe* your model can tell us about social reality.

Box 1   What does a model do?

A model is:

an abstraction from reality that serves the purpose of ordering and simplifying our view of reality while still representing its essential characteristics.... A model, then, is a representation of reality; it delineates certain aspects of the real world as being relevant to the problem under investigation, it makes explicit the significant relationships among the aspects, and it enables the formulation of empirically testable propositions regarding the nature of these relationships. (Frankfort-Nachmias and Nachmias 1992: 44)

A model, like theory, is an abstraction of reality, and can be a good way of visualising some of the relationships between concepts. **Hypotheses** are often depicted using models (i.e. boxes and arrows). The boxes and arrows themselves do not mean anything, except that they depict, in this case, the effect of one variable (let us say a person's dietary intake) on another (let us take level of fitness). If this relationship between two **variables** is written in text, the reader has to imagine it in his or her mind. By using a model, however, the reader receives an abstract picture of the relationship. This becomes more important when you add a list of other factors that may influence a person's level of fitness, for example housing, upbringing, jogs around the block, weight, etc. All of these influences can be schematically laid down to assist our thought processes. You are more likely to come up with other relationships, causal or otherwise, by using a model than if you attempt to store this information in your head.

I think you should avoid conflating the term 'model' with 'research paradigm or tradition' and 'research perspective', as David Silverman does (2000: 77–8). For example, he cites 'functionalism' as a 'model' in social research. To be more precise and less confusing, it is a research 'perspective' in several disciplines, most notably sociology, and it is also a good example of a 'grand theory' (see chapters 5 and 6 for an explanation of 'functionalism'). It falls within a certain 'research paradigm', namely that of 'positivism'. By contrast, a model is a representation of reality imposed on raw data so as to draw out possible relationships among variables.

Typology
Typologies – and, in this rare case, we can use this term interchangeably with 'taxonomies' – are similar systems of classification to ideal types.

They consist of 'a system of categories constructed to fit empirical observations so that relationships among categories can be described' (Frankfort-Nachmias and Nachmias 1992: 40). These devices can be seen as loose frameworks within which to organise and systematise our observations. Typologies do not provide us with explanations; rather they describe empirical phenomena by fitting them into a set of categories. What they do help researchers with is the organisation of a wide range of diverse facts that can be structured into logical, but sometimes arbitrary, categories, which facilitates understanding of complex matters. Bailey sums it up thus: 'One of the chief merits of a typology is **parsimony**. ... A well-constructed typology can work miracles in bringing order out of chaos. It can transform the overwhelming complexity of an apparent eclectic congeries of numerous apparently diverse cases into a well-ordered set of a few rather homogenous types' (cited in Neuman 2000: 44). In comparative politics, the typology has a slightly different role. Built on the earliest classification scheme proposed by Aristotle (see box 2), it serves to 'reduce the complexity of the world by seeking out those qualities that countries share and those that they do not share' (Landman 2000: 5).

Box 2   Aristotle's typology of regime types

Formally speaking, the construction of typologies is the attempt to develop a single variable through the interaction of two or more further variables. And this is exactly what Aristotle did in his attempt to classify regime types:

> by taking the 'form' of rule (either 'good' or 'corrupt') (variable 1) and factoring in the different number of rulers making up the decision-making body (either 'one', 'few' or 'many') (variable 2), Aristotle came up with six different types of regime (variable 3): monarchy, aristocracy and polity (the 'good' regime types) and tyranny, oligarchy and democracy (the 'corrupt' regime types). (for more on this see Heywood 2002: 27–8)

In the more recent literature, analyses are usually statistical in nature and a typology can be seen as an initial stage on the way to theory-building (Peters 1998: 95), and for this reason I have placed this tool before ideal types, which, as we shall see, are similar classificatory tools.

Ideal type

The ideal type is, like theory, a construct that represents an intellectual description of a phenomenon in its abstract form and, like typologies (taxonomies), does not provide us with explanations. It should not be understood as an 'ideal' standard 'in the sense of being perfect, but rather that it is "ideal" in the sense of being an intellectual construct that may never exist in the real world' (Peters 1998: 105). This confusion has arisen to a great extent because of the translation from the German (Blaikie 2000: 165). Attributed to the founder of modern sociology, Max Weber, who was greatly influenced by economic modelling in his day (Weber 1949: 89–90; Ringer 1997: 110–21), an ideal type is a conceptualisation, such as, for example, the 'working class', with which the researcher can compare reality on the ground (empirical evidence). Ideal types are thus hypothetical constructs formed by emphasising aspects of behaviour and institutions which are (generally) empirically observable. These constructs isolate 'those variables central to the study of a problem, putting aside those aspects of the reality which seem inessential to the analysis' (Engerman 2000: 258). An ideal type does not, however, posit relationships among variables. Box 3 gives an abridged version of the classic example of an ideal type: Friedrich's and Brzezinski's categorisation of a totalitarian regime.

Box 3 Ideal type of 'totalitarianism' by Friedrich and Brzezinski, 1956/1965

In this ideal type a totalitarian dictatorship exhibits the following characteristics:

1 An elaborate ideology, consisting of an official body of doctrine covering all vital aspects of man's existence to which everyone living in that society is supposed to adhere.
2 A single mass party typically led by one man, the 'dictator,' and consisting of a relatively small percentage of the total population (up to 10 per cent) of men and women.
3 A system of terror, whether physical or psychic, effected through party and secret-police control, supporting but also supervising the party for its leaders.

Continued

4 A technologically conditioned, near-complete monopoly of control, in the hands of the party and of the government, of all the means of effective mass communication.
5 A similarly technologically conditioned, near-complete monopoly of the effective use of all weapons of armed combat.
6 A central control and direction of the entire economy through the bureaucratic coordination of formerly independent corporate entities. .

They furthermore suggest that 'These six basic features, which we think constitute the distinctive pattern or model of totalitarian dictatorship, form a cluster of traits, intertwined and mutually supporting each other, as is usual in "organic" systems. They should, therefore not be considered in isolation or be made the focal point of comparisons' (Friedrich and Brzezinski, 1956/1965, 21–2).

You can see that this is only a yardstick or **heuristic tool** for analysis, as this particular ideal type has been heavily criticised for its ideological baggage, that is, it comes from a particular ideological angle, and for the way it was employed during the cold war (see Ross and Grix 2002).

Weber himself suggested that the 'ideal typical concept will help develop our skill in imputation in *research*: it *is* no "hypothesis" but it offers guidance to the construction of hypotheses' (Weber 1949: 90).

Box 4   Weber's ideal type

According to Weber an ideal type:

is not a description of reality but it aims to give unambiguous means of expression to such a description.... An ideal type is formed by the one-sided *accentuation* of one or more points of view and by the synthesis of a great many diffuse, discrete, more or less present and occasionally absent *concrete individual* phenomena, which are arranged according to those one-sidedly emphasized viewpoints into a unified *analytical* construct. In its conceptual purity, this mental construct cannot be found empirically anywhere in reality. (Weber 1949: 90)

The 'one-sided' emphasis on specific characteristics in institutions and people is something Weber has become well-known for; for example, his ideal types of 'bureaucracy' and 'charisma' have enjoyed a wide currency among academics.

Paradigm

There are three ways in which the term 'paradigm' is used in the human sciences. The first draws directly on Thomas Kuhn, who depicts a paradigm as an institutionalisation of intellectual activity which, in effect, socialises students into their respective scientific community. Kuhn explains:

> By choosing [the term paradigm], I mean to suggest that some accepted examples of actual scientific practice – examples which include law, theory, application, and instrumentation together – provide models from which spring particular coherent traditions of scientific research .... The study of paradigms ... is what mainly prepares the student for membership in the particular scientific community with which he will later practice. Because he there joins men who learned the bases of their field from the same concrete models, his subsequent practice will seldom evoke overt disagreement over fundamentals. (1996: 10–11)

In the human sciences, the term has come to mean, or is not dissimilar to, 'an established academic approach' in which academics use a common terminology, common theories based on agreed paradigmatic assumptions and agreed methods and practices (see Rosamond 2000: 192). Furthermore, paradigms are often overtaken, replaced or placed alongside other paradigms, leading to what is commonly called a 'paradigm shift'. In academic disciplines, 'dominant' paradigms exist and are often challenged. However, we are not talking about the same kind of 'paradigm' that dominated the natural sciences, as the human sciences are characterised by the plurality of theories that coexist in the many disciplines that make them up (see Dogan 2000: 104–5).

Box 5 Example of a 'paradigm' shift

In macroeconomics the neoclassical paradigm (or 'school of thought') and its world-view has, since the late 1960s/early 1970s, taken over as the dominant approach from its predecessor, Keynesianism. Both of

Continued

---

these paradigms are based on specific ontological and epistemological assumptions which are reflected in the emphasis and priority they place on specific factors, although there is, of course, limited variation on these matters within both paradigms among protagonists. Whilst neoclassical economists advocate the virtues of an unfettered market and a small role for the state, Keynesian approaches usually call for a more active role of the state in stimulating the economy.

Technically, the 'paradigm shift' example above is really talking about 'perspectives' within the study of economics (see chapter 5 for more on this).

The second way in which 'paradigm' is used in research is when students and researchers describe crude and broad groupings of certain **approaches** to the study of a specific topic – for example, on the collapse of communism, the academic literature can be broken down into 'top-down' and 'bottom-up' research paradigms. The former concerns itself with, *inter alia*, power-wielding élites, the latter with the role of citizens in the regimes' maintenance and collapse. Alternatively, you may separate out those approaches which focus on structural explanations of an event and those that focus more on agents (see below for the 'structure–agency problem'). This is a general method of broad categorisation of roughly cognate approaches to specific phenomena – it has little to do with the Kuhnian sense of paradigm in the natural sciences. What it does do is allow you to focus and structure your observations; otherwise, you will end up writing an interesting story without being able to begin to differentiate, at least between the way in which people approach a specific topic.

Finally, the term 'paradigm' is used for describing broad approaches to research, for example the 'positivist' or 'interpretivist' paradigms, within which many academic perspectives draw from similar ontological and epistemological roots. This is the manner in which I have used the term in chapter 5 when I outline key academic perspectives within broad research paradigms (or 'traditions').

Box 6 What's in a paradigm?

You need to differentiate between the following three concepts:
  paradigm: this should be reserved for broad definitions, for

example the 'positivist' paradigm of research (within which there will be vast differences between proponents; see chapter 5)

discipline: this usually applies to 'traditional' academic disciplines like economics, history, political science, etc. (disciplines also contain a multitude of subdisciplines and are not paradigms themselves)

perspective: an academic perspective pertains to (a) certain approaches *within* a discipline, for example, new institutionalism and rational choice in political science, and (b) approaches that transcend narrow academic disciplines, for example, a feminist or post-modern perspective.

Concepts

Concepts are the building blocks of theory, hypotheses, explanation and prediction. A concept can be seen as an idea, or notion, expressed and compressed into one or more words. Concepts represent the least complex stage on our continuum of abstraction. That is not to say that concepts cannot be extremely complex. A concept carries with it a certain perspective and certain built-in assumptions, or ways of looking at empirical phenomena (Neuman 2000: 44), and can be seen as an agreed-upon term among scholars. The agreement, however, is only on the term's existence and not its meaning, as much scholarly debate revolves around precisely this point. A concept is an abstraction of empirical phenomena based on certain assumptions, and can be used as a type of shorthand in explanation. For example, the concept 'book' 'assumes a system of writing, people who can read, and the existence of paper. Without such assumptions, the idea of *book* makes little sense' (Neuman 2000: 44).

Box 7   Take care with concepts: all kinds of 'trust'

The concepts you use in your work usually have referents in the empirical world, so they need to be well defined. If you are interested in say, gauging the level of trust in a specific community, town or country, you would need to be fairly precise about what type of trust you are seeking to uncover. Trust is a multi-faceted concept that, for clarity, is best divided into several subgroups. There are evidently a variety of types of trust that need to be distinguished in order to lend them any operationalisability. For example, interpersonal trust is clearly different from trust in institutions – or perhaps, more precisely,

Continued

> the actors who populate them. Furthermore, the creation of 'generalised trust', trust beyond the individual and group members and extended to strangers, is again different, but not necessarily divorced from, the above two varieties. 'Horizontal' trust between citizens is different from trust between élites and citizens (Grix 2001b: 194–6).

Let us consider the concept cluster 'conditional loyalty', which I used in my own research to capture the relationship between the majority of citizens in the GDR (German Democratic Republic) and the GDR regime. This simple concept was used to suggest that the majority of citizens did not undertake any regime-threatening actions as long as certain 'conditions' were met. My aim was to trace the decline in this 'loyalty' over time and to give reasons for this, all as a way of contributing to an explanation of the regime's collapse (Grix 2000). By developing Albert O. Hirschman's well-known model (see below for more on this), I was able to show how 'loyalty' of citizens to the regime was only 'conditional' on subsidised consumption and by being afforded 'niches' in the dictatorship within which to live reasonably. This short example reveals the work a single conceptual phrase can be made to do and how much information can be packed into it. The key is to be as precise as possible about what you mean by 'conditional', what exactly the conditions are and, of course, what the social, economic and political contexts are in which the action you describe is taking place. **Operationalising** concepts, that is, translating them into measurable variables for data collection, is one of the hardest jobs in research.

Another, more colourful use of concepts is when they are used as a metaphor. Metaphors can be useful in capturing certain characteristics of an institution, country or person. William E. Paterson has made an art form out of employing metaphors to explain Germany's behaviour: he described pre-1990 Germany as a 'Gulliver' (the giant Gulliver in Lilliput) bound by multilateral arrangements and commitments and therefore unlikely to repeat the bellicose behaviour of years previous (Bulmer and Paterson 1989). After German Unification in 1990, Paterson penned an illuminating article entitled 'Gulliver Unbound?', posing the vexing question of whether German unity would take us from a European Germany towards a German Europe (Paterson 1996). You can see how such simple imagery can be used as explanatory tools to capture complex relations between social phenomena.

The abuse of concepts

Researchers must take care not to employ wrongly context-dependent concepts that have been developed at a specific point in time to describe specific phenomena. This can happen if an 'original' concept is referred to by an author, but without her actually revisiting the original texts to substantiate her claims and, importantly, without taking into consideration the changes that may have taken place in the world since the concept was introduced.

Examples abound where concepts and terms have been rendered hollow or extremely hard to define due to this overuse and abuse. Take, for example, the concepts 'stakeholder' and Albert O. Hirschman's schema 'Exit, Voice and Loyalty' which have, to a certain extent, suffered this fate (for the original theory, see Hirschman 1970; for a brief overview, see Grix 2000: 18–22). The use of 'stakeholder' in Britain, which was popularised by Will Hutton (1996; 1999) and the Labour Party, came to mean, among other things, giving a person a stake in society. The term was used so frequently, and in so many different situations, that its original meaning is now somewhat obscured. Albert Hirschman's 'Exit, Voice and Loyalty' scheme, which has been used in as wide a range of settings as social capital (see chapter 4 for an overview of this debate), was reduced simply to 'Exit' and 'Voice' in numerous explanations of the collapse of the German Democratic Republic. The original schema, presented by Hirschman in 1970, is hardly ever referred to, and the third pillar of the scheme, loyalty, is hardly discussed at all (see Grix 2000: 21–2).

Another danger is for concepts to be diluted into a catch-all term like 'civil society', which is impossible to pin down, but regarded as somehow signalling something desirable. The concept of civil society is an interesting one, as it experienced something of a renaissance during the peaceful revolutions of 1989 that marked the beginning of the end of communism. However, the concept has been associated mainly with Western capitalist societies, and simply extending the term to countries transforming from years of dictatorship to some form of democracy is not without its problems. Moreover, it can come across as prescriptive if Western countries state that they will not assist these fledgling democracies until they have a functioning civil society, presumably based on the Western model. This becomes particularly problematic when one considers the differences between countries, their cultures and their citizens who have had to live under dictatorial conditions. How can concepts developed in one cultural, political, economic, social and psychological context capture the complexities of, and be transferred to, another?

The point here is not to suggest that all concepts are context-specific and therefore of not much use outside the region or country for which they were developed. Far from it – the fact that it can transcend boundaries is the mark of a good concept and theory. The point is, however, to make you aware of the danger of *not* considering the origins of a concept (i.e. the context in which it has evolved) and the changes in society since the original concept was introduced.

▶ Key terms in research

The following section continues with the clarification of the language of research by turning to *the* two key terms that are often misunderstood, taken as given – and thus never properly explained – and misused in research.

Methods

At the root of all research lies what the ancient Greeks termed *methodos*. On the one hand, the term means 'the path towards knowledge', and, on the other, 'reflections on the quest for knowledge-gathering'. Many of the central concerns of research have their roots firmly in the work of ancient Greek philosophers. Witness, for example, the manner in which Socrates, Plato and Aristotle employed classificatory systems or typologies of states, types of rule, etc., to make sense of the social phenomena surrounding them.

I follow Norman Blaikie's (2000) more modern definition of **methods** and **methodology**, two words that are often confused, used interchangeably and generally misunderstood (see also Blaxter et al. 1997: 59). The former is easier to explain and understand than the latter. Research methods, quite simply, can be seen as the 'techniques or procedures used to collate and analyse data' (Blaikie 2000: 8). The method(s) chosen for a research project are inextricably linked to the **research questions** posed and to the **sources** of data collected.

Research methods come in all shapes and sizes, ranging from in-depth interviews, statistical inference, discourse analysis and archival research of historical documents to participant observation (see chapter 7 for a brief overview of the most common types of method). The choice of methods will be influenced by ontological and epistemological assumptions and, of course, the questions you are asking, and the *type* of project you are undertaking, e.g. either researching individuals' attitudes or institutional change. However, methods themselves should be seen as *free from ontological and epistemological assumptions*, and the choice of which to use should be guided by your research questions.

Box 8   The link between research questions, methods and sources

If I wish to understand how the policy on a specific issue was made in the European Commission, I would have to think of a way of obtaining information with which to answer this question. One method could be to speak to those who implement policy, or, probably better still, those people who work for key decision-makers in the Commission. In interviews (structured, semi-structured or unstructured – see chapter 7) with key people, I would have to pose questions in such a way as to shed light on the specific area of policy-making in which I was interested. The interviewees may, if I am lucky, point me to specific documents or further discussion partners. Thus, my original question has led me to:

- the interview technique (a research method)
- interview transcripts (raw data derived from interviews)
- (possibly) key documents as source material to analyse (sources of information).

Therefore a research question (RQ) should lead to our method (M) and sources (S) (RQ→M→S). The RQs we ask are guided by our ontological and epistemological positions (see chapter 4).

In the minds of many researchers, certain methods are inextricably bound up with certain ontological and epistemological assumptions: for example, try asking an enthusiastic rational-choice theorist what she thinks of discourse analysis. The important thing to note here is that it is the researcher who employs a particular method in a particular way, thereby associating it with a specific set of ontological assumptions. It is not the method that approaches scholarship with pre-existing baggage, but rather the researcher. However, within the academic community, some methods are looked upon and associated with 'good research', whilst others are not. Remember that good scholarship is not just the result of a specific method, but the result of *how* you employ, cross-check, collate and analyse the data that methods assist you in collecting. Your work should be judged on how its constituent parts logically link together, not by which methods you use.

An advanced undergraduate essay, dissertation or doctoral thesis without any method, however loosely defined, is an out-and-out contradiction. In research, methods have two principal functions:

- They offer the researcher a way of gathering information or gaining insight into a particular issue.
- They enable another researcher to re-enact the first's endeavours by emulating the methods employed.

The former is essential for concentrating and narrowing our line of enquiry when analysing a particular topic. The latter is essential in **validating** research.

Methods can be used in either **quantitative research**, which is concerned predominantly with quantity and quantifying, or **qualitative research**, which is concerned with interpreting the subjective experiences, i.e. the perspectives, of the individuals being studied (see chapter 7 for a further discussion of methods).

Methodology

Methodology is concerned with the logic of scientific enquiry; in particular with investigating the potentialities and limitations of particular techniques or procedures. The term pertains to the science and study of methods and the assumptions about the ways in which knowledge is produced. The difficulty in understanding just what the term 'methodology' means has not been helped by the fact that it is used interchangeably with 'research methods' and is often considered, mistakenly, to be close in meaning to 'epistemology', 'approach' and even 'paradigm'. Epistemology should be looked upon as an overarching philosophical term concerned with the origin, nature and limits of human knowledge, and the knowledge-gathering process itself. A project's methodology, on the other hand, is concerned with the discussion of how a particular piece of research should be undertaken and so can best be understood as the critical study of research methods and their use. The term refers to the *choice* of **research strategy** taken by a particular scholar – as opposed to alternative research strategies. The methodology section of a Master's or doctoral thesis, which is, especially in political science, often replaced with a section on 'ontology and epistemology', has come to mean 'the difficult bit' among students, through which they have to wade before being allowed to go off 'in the field' and enjoy themselves. A student's methodology is driven by certain ontological and epistemological assumptions and consists of research questions or hypotheses, a conceptual approach to a topic, the methods to be used in the study – and their justification – and, consequently, the data sources. All of these components are inextricably linked to one another in a logical manner. The methodology section of a dissertation or thesis embraces, then, the key components: it sets out how you have gone about acquiring the answers to your research questions and/or hypotheses; a discussion of the conceptual approach being adopted, including the research paradigm from which it draws (see chapter 5); the research methods to be used, their limitations and potential and, finally, the sources to be consulted. This is usually the section that can take the most time – especially in postgraduate degrees – as students attempt to place their work among the canon of existing works on their topic, drawing on insights from wide-ranging literature reviews, and developing an 'innovative' angle on events.

▶ Summary

This chapter has been concerned with the pre-research stage, outlining some of the most important tools and terms you should know *before* you begin your research. The major point I have attempted to get across is that familiarity with the tools and terminology of research is essential if you are to complete successfully a high-quality, precise piece of work. Of equal importance is the ability of the researcher to pick and choose *which* conceptual tools to use for her particular project. If you do not know or understand what is on offer, you are unlikely to make the best choice. To sum up the advice of this chapter:

- Take time to learn the 'tools of the trade' (use the glossary at the end of this book).
- Familiarise yourself with the central concepts you are likely to come across in research.
- Reflect on the concepts you are using in your research. Consider their origins and whether they are suitable for the context in which you wish to employ and defend their use. Avoid at all costs the 'abuse of concepts' outlined above.
- Remain aware of the relationship between your research question(s) and the methods and the sources you use.

▶ **Essential reading**

Blaikie, N. (2000) *Designing Social Research*, Cambridge, Polity Press, chapter 1.

Frankfort-Nachmias, C. and Nachmias, D. (1992) *Research Methods in the Social Sciences*, London, Edward Arnold, 4th edn.

Kuhn, T.S. (1996) *The Structure of Scientific Revolutions*, Chicago and London, University of Chicago Press.

▶ **Further reading**

Gerring, J. (2001) *Social Science Methodology. A Criterial Framework*, Cambridge, Cambridge University Press, chapters 1 and 2.

King, G., Keohane, O. and Verba, S. (1994) *Designing Social Inquiry. Scientific Inference in Qualitative Research*, Princeton, NJ, Princeton University Press.

3 Getting Started in Research

Chapter 3 introduces:

- *The language used when getting started in research, including the all-important literature review (x3), research question and hypothesis-building*
- *The key terms and debates to consider when starting research: levels of analysis, structure and agency and types of study*

This chapter introduces the language of getting started in research. It does so by describing the process by which you can begin your research projects. There are various ways of deciding on a topic of study and this chapter will offer examples to help you focus your initial thoughts. The most common of these, the literature review, is given special attention, as everyone has heard of it, but not everyone knows exactly what it is for, and *all* dissertations or theses will have to engage with a body of existing scholarly work. By dissecting the literature review and looking closely at its constituent parts, the aim is to make clear its central purpose in research.

Closely interwoven with the literature review is the process of devising research questions and hypotheses. The purpose of arriving at a more precise research question is to give your study some kind of order and to assist you in narrowing down your topic to something that is manageable within the time you have for your particular degree. Time restrictions are tough, but they can be very good for disciplining your thoughts. This chapter deliberately goes over in detail the terms and terminology associated with hypothesis-building. This is not to advocate a specific type of research or epistemology, but rather to help clarify what is meant by terms such as an 'independent variable'.

The final section turns your attention to the levels and units of analysis in research, which refers, simply, to the technical terms for the 'who' or the 'what' – and at which level: broadly, individual, group or institutional – we are studying. This distinction is important when the researcher starts mixing analyses of individuals and institutions, for findings from one unit or level of analysis cannot straightforwardly be extrapolated to a different unit or level of analysis. After a discussion of the crucial 'structure-agency problem' that all researchers must address, I introduce the two most common types of research you are likely to come across: the case-study and comparative approaches. The idea, once again, is not to give you an in-depth exposition of both types of research, but rather to familiarise you with them and the language used to describe them.

▶ Getting started

The selection of a topic for study will be governed by certain criteria, including the expertise at your host institution, *your personal interest*, and the project's feasibility: that is, the need for the project to be realistic and manageable in the time available. The emphasis here is on *your* interest in a topic, because *you* will be the one dealing with it on a daily basis. However, the first experience of actually having to narrow your focus will probably come with the writing of a dissertation or thesis proposal. This is a very handy exercise in the art of refining and defining exactly what it is you intend to do. It also gives you a rough 'map' to follow in your studies (for an in-depth look at how to construct research proposals, see Punch 2000a). Do remember, however, that original proposals rarely closely resemble the end-product, as research is a to-and-fro of ideas, concepts and data. Here are ten points that should be included in a good, clear research proposal:

1 The context of, and rationale behind, the project (i.e. set the scene and tell the reader *what* it is about by presenting them with a brief background to the topic and setting out your aims).
2 A brief literature review (indicate how the work you propose fits in with current scholarly debates).
3 The methodological approach you will adopt (here you need to give some idea of the theoretical approach you are using) and how your angle on events fits in with the scholars discussed in 2.
4 Research questions and hypotheses (*what* exactly do you wish to find out, or what question do you hope your work will provide an

answer to? Research questions should also point to the level and units of analysis you will use, and the generalisability of the conclusions sought – see the section on case-studies below for more information on this).

5 Your methods of enquiry (in other words, *how*, or by which means, are you going to gather and analyse data? Make sure you indicate how this method sheds light on the questions you have posed).

6 The sources to be employed (what kind of sources are you drawing on?).

7 The significance and utility of the research (i.e. *why* is your project such a wonderful idea?).

8 Any logistical and other difficulties you envisage, and the means of overcoming them.

9 The specific research training required to undertake the project (normally reserved for postgraduate degrees).

10 The timetable of the research.

By setting out the above in great detail, you are well on the way to starting your project. Rarely, however, are the topic or questions contained in an initial research proposal 'sharp' enough for actual research. It is a good idea at this point to be as precise as possible, as questions which are too vague will not help you navigate through the mass of possible information awaiting you. Although there are no hard and fast rules on how to arrive at a precise, narrowly defined and focused statement or research question, there are four very general techniques for helping to refine and focus your initial idea into an achievable and manageable project. I reiterate at this point that the advice of choosing a topic as soon as possible is driven by a sense of pragmatism, and not by any ideological or epistemological preferences.

1 The most common way to begin a substantial piece of research is by undertaking a literature review (sometimes called a literature search), which enables you to 'get a feel for the state of the art' on and around your general topic. It also allows you to assess the feasibility of your project and narrow your likely focus (see the literature review section below for typical sources to draw on).

2 Another way to start is by setting out research questions or hypotheses (for manageability, restrict yourself to three or four), a process which in itself will lead you to the field of study and the correct methods for carrying out the research, including the type and level of analysis necessary, for example systemic, institutional or actor-centred. Bear in mind that research questions should 'contain within

themselves the means for assessing their achievement' (Blaxter et al. 1997: 35). If your questions do not do this, then they are more than likely too general, and need to be sharpened.

3 By refining the key concepts you are employing in your project, you are forced to compare and contextualise. You will thus need to consult the relevant literature to 'place' and compare your concepts with those used in wider academic debates.

4 Another way to get started is to try to sketch out a research proposal or outline on the lines of that proposed above, and ask yourself such questions as 'What might the whole project look like?' and 'How will the thesis eventually be organised?'

You could, of course, mix and match each of the techniques listed above. This is probably what happens in the majority of cases.

The literature review, research questions and hypotheses

Let us consider further the role of a **literature review**, the best-known yet least-understood method of starting a project. Reviewing the secondary literature on a given topic area is common to all dissertations and theses, whether in the social sciences or humanities. The first thing to note is that reviewing the literature is not a compartmentalised stage of research. Instead, the student *constantly* reviews the literature until the day her project is submitted, by which time the last thing she wants to hear about is a newly published study on a relevant topic. The review serves many purposes and is done in many stages. I suggest that there is a continuum which begins at one end with the initial 'dip' into the academic literature and ends, in the period shortly prior to submitting your work, with a 'checking' or 'skimming' of the literature. These two extremes represent two different reasons for reviewing the literature. As you move along the continuum from the initial literature review to the 'skimming' stage, the purpose of the ongoing review changes. These broad stages are discussed further below. Apart from getting you started on your research project, other reasons for reviewing the literature include helping to:

- focus and clarify your research problem (Kumar 1999: 26)
- expose you to, and enable you to demonstrate a familiarity with, the approaches, theories, methods and sources used in your topic area (this is usually a prerequisite of a PhD thesis and a key theme of the viva to which examiners will turn)

- highlight the key debates, terms and concepts employed in your topic area
- acquaint you with the sum of the accumulated knowledge and understanding in a given field and around a particular question or topic, otherwise known as the 'cutting edge' of research
- assist you in identifying a 'gap' in this literature, thereby justifying your particular study's contribution to research, and assisting in your choice of approach and methods
- contextualise your project within a wide-ranging existing knowledge base
- (especially for PhDs) make you an expert in the field of your choice as part of your academic development.

In a literature review you must, above all, make reference to, and engage with, the key texts in your chosen field or on and around your topic. Before you can do this, however, you need to know *where* to look for the literature to review. There are a vast number of places to find literature, including the standard academic sources such as library catalogues and abstracts, CD-ROMs, dissertations and theses, back-issues of relevant scholarly journals (both 'hard copies' and Web-based) and specific documentation centres. So much is now available in this area, and so rapidly are things changing, that it is advisable to get advice from specialist librarians whose job it is to guide users through the maze of complex bibliographical sources. Remember, with Web-based sources you need to note the Web address and the date you downloaded the information. Much of the material on the Web cannot be used for academic purposes, unless it is linked to a recognised journal, dictionary, encyclopaedia (e.g. the *Britannica*) or institution. (On plagiarism see chapter 8.) In addition, there is the relevant secondary literature in scholarly monographs (detailed studies of a single subject) or multi-authored books.

Once you know why you are undertaking a review and where you can locate it, it is time to turn to the 'how'. Three crude stages of the ongoing literature review can be summed up thus: the initial 'dip', the 'hypothesis or research question' stage, and 'the critical review' stage. In between all of these stages, you must find time actually to read whole articles or books, as students under any type of pressure (be it temporal or financial) naturally try to cut corners. An additional type of literature review is the so-called 'skimming' technique, which you can only really undertake once you are already very familiar with a topic and have grasped the core assumptions, arguments and debates contained therein.

The initial 'dip' (stage 1)

At the very start of a project, the best thing to do is undertake an initial review of the academic literature, guided by the 'hunches' you already have or by sheer interest in a topic. During this stage, your 'gut' feelings will quite quickly be confirmed or corrected, which will assist you in gradually acquiring knowledge of your subject, and, more importantly, if it is done correctly, it will give you a broad overview of what has been written already. There is no point in setting a specific time limit for this stage of the review, because everyone works at a different speed and has differential access to material. Suffice it to say, you ought to agree with your tutor or supervisor on a set period of time to undertake this stage. This will differ, depending on the degree which you are taking. For a PhD, for example, six to eight weeks of uninterrupted searching and reading should be sufficient for you to obtain an *overview* of the relevant literature in your field. A good idea is to ask an experienced academic who works in your field for some tips regarding literature. After consulting your supervisor, you could even seek advice by e-mail from someone you do not know personally, as some are happy to help research students, especially those who are copiously citing their work. Academics' addresses, e-mails, and so on can usually be found in your relevant **professional association**'s directory. For example, the *American Political Science Association Directory* and the *Political Science Association/British International Studies Association Directory* have contact details of people in politics and international relations in the US and UK (the same principle applies to most disciplines: simply locate your key association, consider joining it – it usually brings benefits – or visit the association's website). Also, you can use the 'Google' search engine to locate a person and their affiliation in seconds). If you already know someone's academic affiliation, it is usually easy to find their e-mail address from their university's website. Try to get them to guide you to the key texts or articles, including their own work, that you should read. What are, generally speaking, the key debates and approaches to the subject in your field?

Once you have located, photocopied or obtained the key literature around your topic, you can set about reading it. Look carefully at the footnotes in key articles, as this can point you to other major works in your field. You should, even at this early stage, attempt roughly to organise the literature according to different approaches, methods employed and overall conclusions. Once you have consumed the literature you have collected, you are ready to move on to the next stage in the review and in the research process: hypothesis building, or generating research questions.

'Second' literature review, research questions and hypotheses (stage 2)

Before embarking on a full-scale search of everything that has ever been written on your topic, you need to find a way of narrowing your focus. The best way to do this is to go through a process of developing 'hunches' or ideas into **research questions** and/or **hypotheses** to guide your work.

There is no agreed way of arriving at a research question or hypothesis, but most researchers are convinced you do need one to begin the research process (Pennings et al. 1999: 6). Your own interest, ideas, previous research and personal experience will have led you to the academic field on which you wish to concentrate. The initial literature review would have assisted you in selecting a broad topic for study within that field. Now you are ready to set out a *proposition* about your chosen area of study. Although this, again, may seem to chime with a 'positivist' research design discussed in chapter 5, the intention is to assist you in narrowing your focus at an early stage. Do be aware that proceeding this way does not imply that you must *restrict* your overall research focus, for you can adapt and firm up your questions and propositions later in the research process.

In the social sciences in particular, it is considered increasingly necessary for a research question or hypothesis to relate to, and be important for, 'real-world' phenomena (King et al. 1994: 15). In both the humanities and social sciences, the research question should show how it makes a contribution to an existing scholarly literature. Let us take a broad research question as an example. For instance, let's say our area of interest is media representation. Within this huge field of study, we are specifically interested in the representation of Germany in the US media, especially since the Iraq war in 2003. To guide our research initially – and to guide our reading – we could pose the following question: does the media representation of Germany in the US affect American attitudes towards Germany? You need to decide whether you wish to use a research question to guide your work or a more abstract tool, a hypothesis. Do not insist on using hypotheses when a specific research question would do. Both of these tools will assist the research process by guiding your reading in a full-scale literature review, and by helping you select methods and particular sources. It is very important at this stage to decide how you will formulate your research problem, as the latter is 'like the foundation of a building. The type and design of the building is dependent upon the foundation' (Kumar 1999: 35).

A hypothesis is different from a research question in as much as it is usually more closely linked to a theory, and will posit the answer to a research question within itself which will subsequently be 'tested' in fieldwork. The choice of which to use in a study will be governed by the type of study you wish to undertake; for example, a simple research question will suffice for a descriptive study. The research question above could be formulated in a hypothesis, if this were appropriate and if you wished to *explain* rather than describe. From the literature on media representation, you would repeatedly have read about the 'media-effects debate' as being central to any study on the influence of the media. Basically, this debate casts doubt on whether media simply affects 'passive' consumers. Nonetheless, at this early stage, you could posit the tentative proposition – or hypothesis – that, on the whole, negative media coverage of Germany in the US affects Americans' opinion of Germany.

Box 9 What's a hypothesis?

A hypothesis states a relationship between two, or more, concepts and suggests that one has an impact on the other. Verma and Beard sum up a hypothesis and its role in research as: 'A tentative proposition which is subject to verification through subsequent investigation. It may also be seen as the guide to the researcher in that it depicts and describes the method to be followed in studying the problem. In many cases hypotheses are hunches that the researcher has about the existence of relationship between variables' (cited in Bell 1993: 18).

The concepts in the hypothesis need to be *measured* in some way 'in order for the hypothesis to be systematically tested' (Bryman 1995: 6). To convert concepts into measures, often called the 'operationalisation' of concepts in research, the researcher develops variables, which can be understood, simply, as concepts that vary in amount or kind. There are no set ways of finding suitable variables for hypotheses (Bouma and Atkinson 1995: 53), as there is no set way of arriving at a research question or hypothesis in the first place. You need to be aware that such a measure 'is likely to be a relatively imperfect representation of the concept with which it is purportedly associated, since any concept may be measured in a number of different ways, each of which will have its own limitations' (Bryman 1995: 7). There is a danger that, by constructing hypotheses, you gain direction, specificity and focus on the one hand (Kumar 1999: 64) but, on the other, they may divert your attention away from other, potentially interesting 'facets of the data' that you have collected (Bryman and Cramer 1994: 4).

Returning to the example of a hypothesis above, we can now set it out as follows (although, in general, researchers would not use a diagram for a simple two-variable relationship, but would also include a 'control variable' – a variable which is suspected of influencing the variable we really want to study):

Negative media coverage (X)	+	Public attitudes (Y)

This simplified hypothesis states that there is a positive relationship, indicated by the plus sign, between the concepts 'Negative media coverage' and 'Public attitudes'. In this uncomplicated example, the box labelled 'Negative media coverage' is sometimes referred to as the **independent variable** (shown as 'X' in formal models; also depicted as 'IV'). It is also known as 'a causal variable', 'an explanatory variable' and 'an exogenous variable' (Landman 2000: 17), or the thing that 'causes' something else – in this example, change in public attitudes. The latter, sometimes depicted as 'Y' or 'DV' in formal models, is termed the **dependent variable**. Other terms for this include 'outcome variables' or 'endogenous variables' (ibid.: 16), or simply the thing which is 'caused' by the independent variable. It is important to be aware that every dependent variable can be an independent variable, or vice versa: it is the *researcher* who decides where to place the emphasis. So, for example, you could hypothesise that American public attitudes lead to negative media coverage, i.e. turn the above example around.

Your proposition does not need to be set out as above, but schemes and diagrams using boxes and arrows help us visualise the relationships we seek to explore. As a research guide, the above hypothesis is too broad, but what it does do is narrow your reading further and pose a number of important questions which will impact on how you proceed with your work: which type of media do you mean? Over what period? What do you mean by public attitudes? and so on. This helps you find answers to these questions by returning to the relevant literature you used for your initial 'dip'.

A further exploratory literature review could result in unpacking the following debates or strands of research:

- works concerning media coverage in general in the US
- works discussing the variety of specific media coverage of Germany in the US (print media, television, radio, internet)
- American public attitudes towards other countries, in particular Germany
- the variety of disciplinary approaches to this topic, ranging from media studies and communication studies to political science, area studies and sociology.

From this breakdown of literature on and around our example, three broad areas of research can be distinguished, under the first three points of the list above. The next task is to focus further still on the area you wish to study by sharpening the hypothesis in the light of the literature search above. The period of study has to be manageable, so, for this example, you could select one specific type of media and a three-year period, leading to the following hypothesis:

US print media coverage of Germany (X)	+	US public attitudes towards Germany (Y)

The period of study is now 2000–03 and the **working hypothesis** – that is, a provisional conjecture to guide the investigation which will be refined in the light of further reading and research – is that the US print media coverage of Germany has an impact on and influences US public attitudes towards Germany.

Full-scale critical literature review (stage 3)
After the above revision of the hypothesis, you are ready to undertake a thorough review of the literature, which will enable you to:

- become further acquainted with the literature on your chosen topic
- gain insight into the key debates and major questions on US print media coverage of Germany and US public attitudes towards Germany
- confirm your initial hypothesis or hunch that 'X' has a positive impact on 'Y'

- learn how other, more experienced researchers analyse the subject and which theories, methods and sources they employ
- sharpen and narrow your focus of enquiry further to particular types of media or newspapers
- reassure yourself that there is not already a wealth of literature positing exactly the same hypothesis.

Box 10   The literature review: an ongoing, reflexive process

Remember the literature review has different purposes at different times during your project. I have identified three key stages:

1   The 'dip' into the literature in order to get a feel for what has and crucially what has not been written about your topic area.
2   The RQ or hypothesis-building stage: you should now be in a position to narrow your focus of literature significantly from 1 above. The purpose here is to finish with general RQs or tentative hypotheses (maximum of three or four for manageability).
3   The critical literature review, undertaken with your RQ(s) and hypothesis in mind. Refrain from simply listing the books, articles and proponents who have dealt with your topic area. Give a clear indication of their strengths, weaknesses and how they fit with your ideas and approach.

As I have mentioned before, you need to conceive the literature review as an *ongoing, reflexive process*, just like the whole research process itself. By this I mean that the constituent parts which make up the literature review and your whole project are *constantly* revisited throughout the period of study. You need to consider each and every stage of the research process in the light of the preceding and subsequent stage and how one impacts on, or connects with, the other. The critical literature review outlined above, is, however, crucial to the beginning of research, as it sets the parameters for your project.

Postgraduate students have to locate their approach *vis-à-vis* other scholars in the field, and they have to justify why their chosen approach is better suited to the task than any other. A good way of achieving this, and structuring your first chapter, is to set out the review according to 'different approaches, interpretations, schools of thought or subject areas' (Blaxter et al. 1997: 112) – this is akin to the use of 'paradigms' advocated in chapter 2. There are many benefits of such an approach. It not only sets up the argument in the light of other researchers' work, but also shows the reader that you are more than aware of the range of literature in your field. The critical reading of works dealing with your chosen topic also has the benefit of drawing attention to their strengths and weaknesses, allowing you to 'position' yourself against the rest, to offer some further justification for the approach chosen, and to indicate to the reader your take on events.

You should avoid developing a 'thinly disguised annotated bibliography' (Hart 2000: 1) in the place of a proper, and critical, review of the literature. The purpose is to engage with the current literature, and to use it to develop your own approach and argument by critically analysing and flagging up the ideas you find fruitful or not. You should be looking to 'note any controversies in this literature, explain their origins and evolution, detail the arguments made by both sides, and summarize their current status' (Van Evera 1997: 101). You should not be presenting the reader with a giant book review, simply regurgitating in the form of a synopsis the contents of each book you have laid your hands on. Such a structured approach as outlined above can give order to the array of diverse literature available on your topic (see Hart 2000: 10), which can range from a wide variety of disciplines and discourses to different types of text, i.e. serious academic monographs or journalistic accounts, to 'officially' produced material of firms, associations, political parties and print media.

After undertaking a literature review with the revised hypothesis in mind, to discipline your reading further, you can now return to the drawing board and redefine your proposition. By now, you will be aware of the key approaches in your respective fields or areas of study. At this point, you should reflect on the appropriateness of the mainstream approaches for their questions and projects and you should not shy away from *developing different approaches* or a mix of different approaches, drawing on different variables to test your hypotheses – providing the ontological and epistemological positions of the approaches are compatible (see chapter 4 for a full discussion of this). Here, the importance of having a research question or hypothesis will become apparent, for in order to choose the most appropriate approach or theoretical framework to organise the data, you need to be clear about the 'what' and 'why' questions. In the example, I have chosen media representation of Germany in the US (the 'what'), and narrowed this down to newspaper coverage of Germany between 2000 and 2003 as my independent variable, or the thing which causes or affects US public attitudes towards Germany in the hypothesis. Thus, I need to decide on the exact newspaper titles to concentrate on and find a way of measuring their impact on attitudes towards Germany. I also need to explain what I mean by attitudes, media effects and media influence. Basically, I need to establish whether (increasing) negative reportage of Germany has been accompanied by a rise in negative attitudes towards Germany. If this can be established, then I could suggest there is a **correlation** between 'increasing negative reportage of Germany' and 'worsening attitudes towards Germany' (i.e. X impacts on Y). As you can see, once you start to unpick the question or hypothesis, it has a whole number of implications for how you are going to attempt to answer, validate or refute it (for a thorough discussion on refuting or 'falsifying' hypotheses, see Popper 2000: 27–48 and Bell 1993: 70). The next stage of research is inherent in the question or hypothesis you are posing: what *level* and *unit* of analysis are you going to use? And what *type* of approach and *method* of empirical research will you choose?

▶ Levels of analysis and types of research

Something all students and scholars eventually come up against is the question of levels of analysis (for the specific 'levels of analysis problem' in international relations, see Hollis and Smith 1990: 7–9). If you have a decent research question or hypothesis, as you should have, this will point you to the *level* of analysis you are going to research – including the structure–agency problem – and the *type* of study you are going to undertake. The following deals with each of these three areas in turn.

Levels of analysis
The level of analysis on which you focus will be linked to the units of analysis you choose. Units can include individuals, groups, organisations, and social categories and institutions (Neuman 2000: 134), the exact choice of which will impact on the methods and sources used in your study. The thing to remember with units of analysis is that each has 'unique attributes; thus it is often misleading to shift from one unit to another. Generalizations based on individuals as units of analysis and generalizations based on groups can be quite different' (Frankfort-Nachmias and Nachmias 1992: 53).

It is possible to mix units of analysis, but you need to distinguish between them in the study and remain aware of their relationship with the level at which you are operating. In this way, you will avoid a mismatch between units: that is, attempting to explain something on an individual level by drawing conclusions from findings relating to aggregate data, in other words, a different level of analysis. In research-methods textbooks this is referred to as the 'ecological fallacy' (Neuman 2000: 136), but has little to do with tree-hugging and environmental preservation. Adopting different levels of analysis in the same case-study can, however, offer a richer account of a specific event by employing different 'lenses through which to view phenomena' (Robins 1995: 69), which are based on different assumptions. As a consequence, 'the level of analysis determines what evidence is considered permissible and hence guides the fieldwork process and underscores the way in which the data are ultimately interpreted' (ibid.: 69). Two common levels of analysis in the human sciences are the:

- **micro**-level, individual or actor-centred
- **macro**-level, system or structure-centred.

A straightforward study of why individuals vote for a particular political party could focus on the individuals themselves, asking them, by way of a questionnaire or interview, why they voted for party X, Y or Z (micro-level). If, however, you wished to include an analysis of how particular parties attract voters, your analysis would have to shift to an organisational level (macro-level). There is no problem with including all sorts of levels of analysis in your study, sometimes called a 'multi-level analysis' (Pennings et al. 1999: 9), as long as you distinguish clearly throughout your work the level with which you are dealing.

The structure and agency problem

In much social research, there appears to be a divide between those scholars who 'believe all of politics can be explained by focusing on micro-level processes' and those who 'believe that all of politics can be explained by a focus on macro-level processes' (Landman 2000: 17). The debate about whether to focus on structure or agency in research touches on a much wider, and unsolvable, ontological puzzle in the human sciences which has become known, simply, as the **structure and agency problem** (see Hay 1995). Briefly, and simplistically, this dilemma revolves around the puzzle of whether it is the social context in which individuals act that guides, determines, constrains or facilitates their actions, or whether it is the individuals (or actors) themselves who form and shape the social context and institutions around them.

Box 11 What's the structure and agency problem?

It is, according to Stuart McAnulla, as follows:

Fundamentally, the debate concerns the issue of to what extent we as actors have the ability to shape our destiny as against the extent to which our lives are structured in ways out of our control; the degree to which our fate is determined by external forces. Agency refers to individual or group abilities (intentional or otherwise) to affect their environment. Structure usually refers to context; to the material conditions which define the range of actions available to actors. (2002: 271)

In the academic literature there are a number of different ways of viewing the structure–agency problem: some, like Anthony Giddens, suggest that structure and agency form a 'duality' and are one and the same. This has been articulated most extensively in his 'theory of structuration' (Giddens 1979). Others tend not to share this notion of mutual dependency between structure and agency, but opt rather for an understanding of structure and agency as two separate entities (i.e. a 'dualism' instead of a 'duality'), that are nonetheless inextricably bound up with one another (Archer 1995; Sibeon 1999). Colin Hay (building on the work of Bob Jessop) takes the debate further by elegantly formulating a 'strategic–relational' approach that suggests that structure and agency are mutually constitutive, as Giddens suggests, but they can be treated as separate for analytical purposes. This means that Hay's conception of structure and agency can be employed in actual research, whereas 'structuration theory' presents great problems when applied to empirical phenomena (see McAnulla 2002: 279). For this reason, Hay suggests that

> structure and agency are best seen, not so much as flip-sides of the same coin, as metals in the alloy from which the coin is forged. From our vantage-point [that of the strategic–relational approach] they do not exist as themselves but through their relational interaction. Structure and agency, though analytically separable, are in practice completely

interwoven (we cannot see either metal in the alloy only the product of their fusion). (Hay 2002: 127)

It is important to remember that issues of structure and agency are ontological in nature and Hay's example above is a clearer rendition of the at times dense work of Roy Bhaskar (Archer et al. 1998: 203; see the glossary and, in particular, the example of a critical-realist ontology in chapter 4). As such, there is no 'correct' answer to whether you should focus more on agents or structures in your studies. The balance of emphasis will be related directly to your ontological position and you should attempt to make this explicit in your work. In chapter 4 we shall discuss several examples of how a scholar's ontological position affects the rest of her **research strategy**, including the objects of study on which she focuses.

▶ Types of study

A variety of types of study are available to the researcher and the choice will, once again, relate directly back to what it is you want to know, what you think it is possible to know and what there is to know about (i.e. your ontological position). The most common types are the **case-study** approach and the comparative approach (in general, these two types of study incorporate other types of study, for example 'historical', 'descriptive' or 'action'; see Walliman 2001: 88 for an overview of these and others). Case-studies are by far the most popular form of study at postgraduate level and are necessarily included in comparative analyses that compare cases, usually across countries. Broadly speaking, there are three types of case-study (Yin 1994: 1):

- descriptive
- exploratory
- explanatory.

The first generally applies to a dissertation or thesis with a more historical subject. Its aim is not to explain the influence or impact of certain factors in the event on which it is focusing, but to give a detailed account of a particular issue, person or process. An exploratory case-study, on the other hand, is usually carried out with the intention of testing initial working hypotheses, checking for availability of, and access to, relevant data, ascertaining the relevant variables for a study and assessing the suitability of the case for further, more extensive, research. A mini-exploratory case-study is usually a good idea for research degrees, because you need to be sure you are asking the right questions, have chosen the correct case to study, and are likely to have some data with which to answer your questions, before you commit yourself to a long period of **fieldwork**. The explanatory case-study is perhaps the most common in the social sciences, in which researchers seek to make generalisations by extrapolating the single case-study's findings to other cases (see below).

Yin, the most cited writer on the topic, defines a case-study as an 'empirical inquiry that investigates a contemporary phenomenon within its real-life context, especially when the boundaries between phenomenon and context are not clearly evident' (ibid.: 13). The emphasis on context is crucial, as the rationale for honing in on a specific case is to be able to identify, uncover and unpick specific contextual factors in which the event, person or policy you are analysing is embedded. Once you have decided that the case-study approach is the best way forward, you need to ask yourself whether a single (in-depth) case-study is suitable or maybe a series of case-studies, referred to, simply, as a 'multiple' case-study. Single, in-depth case-studies are the usual format for UG dissertations, MAs and, increasingly, for many PhD theses (usually because this makes the projects more feasible), which is fine providing students display an awareness of wider theoretical and methodological issues.

Box 12 Single case-studies

A single case-study is a very specific approach to phenomena 'through thorough analysis of an individual case' (Kumar 1999: 99). The subject of such a case could be anything from an individual, a town, a group or political party, a region or community, a specific process, decision or policy, and so on. Case-studies are not tied to any particular research method and they are not 'methods' themselves, but instead should be seen as simply an organisational strategy, within which social data are organised 'so as to preserve the unitary character of the social object being studied' (Goode and Hatt 1952, cited in Punch 2000a: 150).

To assist in deciding whether a case-study approach is best for you, look carefully at the manner in which experienced researchers in your field have set about their analyses, whilst bearing in mind that the aim is to produce something original and distinctive. It is very common for students to begin their studies with more case-studies than they end up doing. Remember, if you are not undertaking a comparative study, it is better to do one case properly, than to skim over five or six without being able to probe deeply enough to uncover anything worthwhile. In the social-science community, single case-studies have tended to be looked down upon, chiefly because of their lack of generalisability, though this objection is no longer made as strongly as it once was. In box 13 Punch offers positive reasons why single cases are valuable in research.

Box 13 Positive reasons for using single cases

The first is what we can learn from the study of a particular case, in its own right... the case being studied might be unusual, unique or not yet understood, so that building an in-depth understanding of the case is valuable.... Second, only the in-depth case study can provide understanding of the important aspects of a new or persistently problematic research area.... Discovering the important features, developing an understanding of them, and conceptualizing them for further study, is often best achieved through the case study strategy. (Punch 2000b: 155–6)

One in-depth case-study of a relatively under-researched area can be embedded in, and compared with, the existing body of literature and studies to gain useful insights into a particular region or to establish similar patterns between well-researched regions and the chosen study. In-depth studies are also capable of contributing to the advancement of specific theories (Ragin 1994: 46), especially if local or regional specificities can be shown to have relevance for, or to be similar to, causes and effects inherent in incidences or events beyond the territorial limits of the original case-study. Researchers must be aware, however, not to 'immerse themselves wholly in the case study details' (Blaxter et al. 1997: 66), but must instead ensure their study is embedded in, and connects with, a wider body of academic research.

It goes without saying that the type of case-study you choose will impact greatly on the methods you employ and the data you collect. If, for example, you do an in-depth study of a particular town, analysing the role of civic engagement in facilitating local democracy, you will be able – depending on the degree you are doing and the time you have to do it – to speak to the majority of civic leaders who matter, to local councillors and to other town dignitaries. To supplement your élite-level interviews, you could analyse the relevant articles on participatory politics in the local press and gather statistics relevant for the town (e.g. How many people use their right to vote? How many people take part in extra-parliamentary action and how often?). Here you can see it would appear relatively easy to collect the data necessary for covering such a topic in a single town or region. To add even more value to such a study, although this is not always necessary, it would be good to do exactly the same for a different town, which perhaps has a similar history (let us say both towns used to be busy harbours), but which, in contrast with the other, flourishes economically. By dipping into the research toolbox discussed above, you can set about categorising why town A fares better than town B and what impact, for example, levels of civic participation have on local economic growth rates. Try repeating the above example over ten cases and you would be in trouble, first, intellectually, as local, social, economic and political contexts differ so much that such a wide comparison would be hard to maintain, and secondly, financially, as such an exercise would demand considerable resources. You cannot possibly interview 500 people in addition to gathering supplementary information. The time required to set up, and carry out, let alone analyse, that number of interviews, would take you way beyond the temporal limits allowed for undergraduate dissertations, MAs or even PhDs.

Comparative studies

Most comparative-research textbooks emphasise the fact that people compare things on a daily basis, as they set about distinguishing between sizes ('big', 'bigger') and types ('different', 'the same'). It is very hard, if not impossible, to undertake any form of quantitative or qualitative research without resorting to some sort of comparison, because most of our judgements are checked against previous experience and knowledge which we bring with us to the research situation. Whilst this intuitive comparison takes place constantly, 'comparative studies' can be seen as a specific *type* of study, especially within political science.

Comparative studies have to involve more than one case, by definition, be it the same subject for study across time or a number of separate subjects. Comparison can take place on a case-by-case basis, for example using in-depth studies to compare French drinking habits with those of the British, or both countries' welfare systems (fieldwork for the former may be more interesting than the latter!). Cross-national comparisons usually involve the researcher measuring variables across a number of nations.

Box 14 The comparative rationale

The rationale behind comparative studies can be understood as the following (based on examples in Landman 2000: 4–10):

- To provide contextual knowledge about other countries, their systems of governance, and so on. By comparing, the researcher places his or her own country or system in a wider context, whilst drawing out similarities or differences between countries produces further information and knowledge.
- Linked with the discovery of similarities or differences, the notion of classification, touched on above, whereby the comparative researcher attempts to arrive at a typology of countries, electoral systems, welfare states, and so on.

The final two, interlinked, reasons behind comparative studies are:

- hypothesis testing
- prediction.

The former consists of developing a hypothesis to be tested in cross-comparison analyses, something deemed by some as a prerequisite for the starting point of any comparative study (Pennings et al. 1999: 6). The latter is the harder job to undertake – the researcher attempting 'to make claims about future political outcomes' (Landman 2000: 10) based on generalisations derived from a comparison of several countries.

Indicators such as GNP (gross national product) or statistics referring to births, deaths, age, etc., are converted into variables and analysed using statistical analysis. If your comparison is to be cross-national and you intend drawing on sources other than statistics, you need to think seriously about language, as you would be, in effect, interpreting the interpretations of others. Relying on scant English language coverage may be acceptable for undergraduate dissertations, but it is not ideal as a source base for postgraduate degrees. The level of written and spoken language competence needed for such degrees will depend very much on the type of study you undertake and the methods you employ.

Box 15 It's natural to compare

Comparison, according to Pennings et al. can be seen as:

one of the most important cornerstones of the development of knowledge about society and politics and insights into what is going on, how things develop and, more often than not, the formulation of statements about why this is the case and what it may mean to all of us. In short, comparisons are part and parcel of the way we experience reality and, most importantly, how we assess its impact on our lives and that of others. (1999: 3)

As suggested above, typologies are frequently used in comparative research as a tool with which to compare cases. Typologies are often derived in the first instance from comparing a variety of cases, noting the chief characteristics and listing them. It is this list which can be used as a sort of device with which to study further cases. Without labelling it as such, most academics categorise, classify and sort out the information they have gathered, in order to compare it and, ultimately, to make sense of it.

▶ Summary

Chapter 3 has been concerned with the language and process of 'getting started' in research, perhaps one of the hardest stages for first-time researchers. One of the key lessons to be learnt from this chapter is the inherent *logic* of the research process; that is, how the literature review leads us quite naturally to define and refine our area of study and points us to specific research questions or hypotheses, which in turn lead us to our level of analysis and type of study. To sum up:

- The literature review is an ongoing process which can be (artificially) divided into three stages: the 'dip' stage, the 'hypothesis or research question' stage and the 'critical review' stage.

- You should use research questions or hypotheses as guides to your reading and research, but remain aware that these same guides may point you away from some important factors.
- Regardless of whether you study three cases in one town, or three towns in one country, or whether you compare one country with three others, you need to be aware of how the *type* of study you are doing links with the *level* and *unit* of analysis you choose and the degree of generalisability of your conclusions. You need to justify and defend your views on this.
- Importantly, you need to make sure that these types, levels and units are the correct ones to shed light on the research questions you wish to answer or the hypotheses you aim to validate or refute.
- You need to reflect carefully on the structure and agency problem and remain aware of the claims you are making in your projects.
- You should remain reflexive throughout the whole process described above, as initial assumptions or 'gut feelings' may need to be re-examined.

▶ Essential reading

Hart, C. (2000) *Doing a Literature Review*, London, Sage.
Hay, C. (2002) *Political Analysis*, Basingstoke, Palgrave Macmillan, chapter 3.
Punch, K. F. (2000b) *Developing Effective Research Proposals*, London, Thousand Oaks, CA and New Delhi, Sage.
Yin, R. K. (1994) *Case Study Research. Design and Methods*, London, Thousand Oaks, CA and New Delhi, Sage, 2nd edn.

▶ Further reading

Kumar, R. (1999) *Research Methodology. A Step-By-Step Guide for Beginners*, London, Thousand Oaks, CA and New Delhi, Sage.
Landman, T. (2000) *Issues and Methods in Comparative Politics. An Introduction*, London and New York, Routledge.
Pennings, P., Keman, H. and Kleinnijenhuis, J. (1999) *Doing Research in Political Science. An Introduction to Comparative Methods and Statistics*, London, Thousand Oaks, CA and New Delhi, Sage.
Punch, K. F. (2000a) *Introduction to Social Research. Quantitative and Qualitative Approaches*, London, Thousand Oaks, CA and New Delhi, Sage.

4 The Building Blocks of Research

In this chapter we turn to the very foundations of research by discussing:

- The concepts of ontology and epistemology
- The need to be clear about the issues they raise
- The impact they have on the rest of the research process
- The 'directional' relationship between ontology, epistemology, methodology, methods and sources

Ontology and **epistemology** are to research what 'footings' are to a house: they form the foundations of the whole edifice. Now, according to many, there is no need for us to worry about such footings, as this is best left to philosophers and the like, who have time to dwell on the theories of being and knowledge. I take a different view. If we are to present clear, precise and logical work, and engage and debate with others' work, then we need to know the core assumptions that underlie their work and inform their choice of research questions, methodology, methods and even sources. Furthermore, we need to realise that we can't chop and change between ontologies and epistemologies as we see fit, because (a) many combinations are not logical and (b) to paraphrase Marsh and Furlong (2002), your research foundations are a skin, not a sweater to be changed every day.

According to Clough and Nutbrown (2002: 30), if students, in their work, were to 'elaborate [their] ontological and epistemological background, then the wheel would truly be endlessly re-invented'. Apparently, it is a waste of time to clarify your research 'footings', because it has been done before by others in different pieces of work. Following this logic, they insist further that 'if we examine any piece of empirical research, it is clear that there is at work a great many assumptions about what the world is, how it works and how we can claim to know these things'. This is not the case if the work under examination follows their advice, as an answer to such questions can only be given with reference to the 'footings' that we should seek to make explicit. There are several reasons for wanting to have a clear and transparent knowledge of the ontological and epistemological assumptions that underpin research:

1 To understand the interrelationship of the key components of research (including methodology and methods).
2 To avoid confusion when discussing theoretical debates and approaches to social phenomena.
3 To be able to recognise others', and defend our own, positions.

I should like to dwell on these points. Why is clarity and constancy of terms so important? If we, as researchers, are unclear about the onto-logical and epistemological basis of a piece of work, we may end up criticising a colleague for not taking into account a factor which her ontological position does not allow for. For example, criticising a full-blown positivist for not taking into account hidden structures in society (e.g. patriarchal structures), when her ontological and epistemological position does not allow for such things, is a classic case of arguing past one another. Achieving such clarity in research presumes not only familiarity with academic terms on our part, but also that researchers whose work we read are explicit about their own ontological and epis-temological positions. Ontology and epistemology can be considered as the foundations upon which research is built. Methodology, methods and sources are closely connected to and built upon our ontological and epistemological assumptions.

Box 16   Beware ontological inconsistencies

Clough and Nutbrown offer the extraordinary advice: 'many researchers ... do not select one research paradigm to investigate all their questions, choosing *either* a normative *or* interpretive approach. In our own work we have – during the course of our research careers – worked within both positivist and interpretivist paradigms .... The important point here is that we adopt research stances as they are appropriate to our work' (2002: 19, emphasis in original).

This chapter will go some way in attempting to convince you that our 'footings' should be treated as something that can not simply be picked up or dropped as we fancy; for example, on a Tuesday we are researching as a positivist, but by Friday we have become an interpretivist. This is done by, first, offering a discussion of the key terms 'ontology' and 'epistemology' and then presenting the thesis of a 'directional relationship' between the key components of research (namely ontology, epistemology, methodology, methods and even sources), building on and out from previous work on such a relationship (in particular Hay 2002: 61–5 and Grix 2002b).

To show how this works in practice, how a particular ontological position impacts on and affects the subsequent stages of research, I give the example of the current debate around the term 'social capital'.

▶ Ontology

Ontology is the starting point of all research, after which one's epistemological and methodological positions logically follow. A dictionary definition of the term usually describes it as 'the image of social reality upon which a theory is based', not a great deal of help to those of us seeking clarity. Blaikie (2000: 8) offers a fuller definition, suggesting that ontological claims are 'claims and assumptions that are made about the nature of social reality, claims about what exists, what it looks like, what units make it up and how these units interact with each other. In short, ontological assumptions are concerned with what we believe constitutes social reality' (Blaikie 2000: 8). With this in mind, it is not difficult to understand how different scholarly traditions embedded in fundamentally different cultural contexts can have diverging views of the world and differing assumptions underpinning their particular approaches to social enquiry. For the current discussion it is important to make you aware of the need to *understand, acknowledge* and *defend* your own ontological position.

Box 17   What's an ontological position when I see one?

An individual's ontological position is their:

answer to the question: what is the nature of the social and political reality to be investigated? Alternatively, what exists that we might

Continued

> acquire knowledge of?... this is a rather significant question and one whose answer may determine, to a considerable extent, the content of the... analysis we are likely to engage in and, indeed, what we regard as an (adequate)... explanation. (Hay 2002: 61)

Your ontological assumptions, as described above, are impossible to refute empirically (see also Hughes and Sharrock 1997: 5–6). It is only after the questions in box 17 have been asked that one can discuss what it is that we can know about this social and political reality that is thought to exist (see epistemology below). Some authors wrongly conflate 'ontology' and 'epistemology' and even suggest that there is no 'sense in which one is, logically or otherwise, prior to the other' (Jenkins 2002: 6). I argue that 'ontology' is logically prior to 'epistemology' and the two concepts must be kept apart, although, as we shall see, they are inextricably linked.

Box 18 Why do we need to know about 'ontology'?

Lewis (2002: 17) succinctly sums up the reasons for getting to grips with our ontology:

It is impossible to engage in any sort of ordered thinking about the political [or social] world without making a commitment (if only implicitly) to some sort of social ontology, because any attempt to conceptualise political phenomena inevitably involves the adoption of some picture of the nature of social being. Explicit reflection about ontological issues can help clarify the precise character of theoretical positions and arguments. This is useful in a number of ways: it allows intuitions to be more fully articulated and developed; *it helps to reveal internal inconsistencies in arguments; and it enables researchers to identify more accurately the differences between competing approaches* (my emphasis).

Your 'ontological position', whether you know it or not, is implicit even before you choose your topic of study. We all have views on how the world is made up and what the most important components of the social world are. Many students get stuck at this point, unable to see why we should be bothering with something so abstract as the nature of social 'reality'. However, as you shall see, it is only with a clear under-standing and recognition that a wide variety of ontological positions actually exist and can lead to different research results, that we can begin to engage with other scholars' work. As Mason (1998: 12–13) rightly points out, a 'reluctance to address these issues [often] stems from vagueness, imprecision, or a failure to understand that there is more than one ontological perspective'.

Box 19 Ontological positions

Ontological positions are often divided between those based on foun-dationalism and those based on anti-foundationalism. Foundationalism believes that 'true knowledge must rest upon a set of firm, unques-tionable ... indisputable truths from which our beliefs may be logically deduced, so retaining the truth value of the foundational premises from which they follow' (Hughes and Sharrock 1997: 4–5).

Central to a foundationalist view is that reality is thought to exist independently of our knowledge of it. As we shall see in chapter 5, this is the starting point for positivist and realist traditions of research. Also, this camp believe that there are central values that exist which can be rationally and universally grounded (Flyvbjerg 2001: 130). On the other hand, anti-foundationalists do not believe that the world exists inde-pendently of our knowledge of it, but rather 'reality' is socially and dis-cursively 'constructed' by human actors. They also believe that there are no central values that can be rationally and universally grounded.

These two starting points are important because of the interrela-tionship of the key components of research: ontology, epistemology, methodology and methods. Thus certain ontological positions *are likely* to lead to certain epistemological positions.

Examples of ontological positions are those contained within the umbrella terms 'objectivism' and 'constructivism'. Broadly speaking, the former is 'an ontological position that asserts that social phenomena and their meanings have an existence that is independent of social actors'. The latter, on the other hand, is an alternative ontological position that 'asserts that social phenomena and their meanings are continually being accomplished by social actors. It implies that social phenomena and categories are not only produced through social interaction but that they are in a constant state of revision' (all from Bryman 2001: 16–18). It is clear from these two examples how your ontological position will affect the manner in which you undertake research (see below for a more detailed discussion on this).

Box 20 A critical-realist ontology in action: The job seeker's strategy

Let's borrow the example of a job seeker from McAnulla (2002: 281) and embellish it somewhat. The case of the jobseeker helps us illuminate the importance of the strategy of individuals within structure and agency in social research, given, as I have pointed out in chapter 2, that it is an ontological matter. Let us suppose that our job seeker has had a string of unsuccessful attempts at getting a job due to certain 'structural' disadvantages she suffers. Let us further suppose that this agent undertakes a job-seeking strategy with the purpose of altering the factors that prevented her obtaining gainful employment in the first place. Through feedback from potential employers and interviews, she finds out that her shabby appearance, bad breath and lack of relevant qualifications have all played a major part in her not being taken on. This agent takes further action by sorting out her wardrobe, flossing and polishing her teeth and obtaining some relevant qualifications. Now, let's say this person gets a job: this would be as a result of her own agency within structural parameters that hitherto constrained her from obtaining employment, but which she had now altered in her favour. This example assumes, in the interest of clarity, passive structures. It could be the case, of course, that the demand for French-polishers, which our agent has now qualified herself as, is no longer as high as it was, making finding a job more difficult.

The term 'ontology' has a number of different meanings in different fields of enquiry; the definition outlined above is nearer to that used in philosophy meaning a system of categories that make up a particular vision of the world, although this discipline distinguishes among a number of varieties of ontology (formal, descriptive, etc.). In the fields of artificial intelligence, neurophysiology, psychology and cognitive science much work has been done on how the brain understands the world around us. The brain, it is suggested, divides the world up into 'ontological categories' (plants, animals, tools, persons and natural objects) so that it can understand its environment (Grayling 2002: 21). It is at this point that the philosophical and psychological/physiological examples meet: categorisation and conceptualisation of the social world (or how we interpret the 'nature of social reality'). People who share similar academic perspectives tend to draw from similar world-views and use similar terminology to describe and 'capture' the social world.

If ontology is about what we may know, then epistemology is about how we come to know what we know.

▶ Epistemology

Turning to a trusty dictionary to get to the bottom of this term will offer as much clarification as the 'ontology' example above. Formally, epistemology is one of the core branches of philosophy concerned with the theory of knowledge, especially in regard to its methods, validation and 'the possible ways of gaining knowledge of social reality, whatever it is understood to be. In short, claims about how what is assumed to exist can be known' (Blaikie 2000: 8). Derived from the Greek words *episteme* (knowledge) and *logos* (reason), epistemology focuses on the knowledge-gathering process and is concerned with developing new models or theories that are better than competing models and theories.

Box 21 Enigmatic epistemology

Richard Jenkins offers a few reasons why the term 'epistemology' has become shrouded in mystery: 'Partly due to its other life as a branch of scholastic philosophy, and partly due to the prolix navel-gazing that has, for several decades now, been the reflexive norm for too many social theorists, the very word 'epistemology' is capable of striking terror into the hearts of professionals and students alike' (Jenkins 2002: 91).

Knowledge, and the ways of discovering it, is not static, but forever changing. When reflecting on theories, and concepts in general, students need to reflect on the assumptions on which they are based and where they originate from in the first place. For example, can theories generated in Western democracies properly explain phenomena in east European transition states with a 60-year history of authoritarianism? Two contrasting epistemological positions are those contained within the research paradigm, "positivism" and "interpretivism". These terms can be traced back to, and illuminated by reference to, specific traditions in the philosophy of human sciences (as they are in chapter 5). Broadly speaking, the former 'is an epistemological position that advocates the application of the methods of the natural sciences to the study of social reality and beyond'. The latter, on the other hand, can be seen as an epistemological position that 'is predicated upon the view that a strategy is required that respects the differences between people and the objects of the natural sciences and therefore requires the social scientist to grasp the subjective meaning of social action' (all from Bryman 2001: 12–13). It is clear that choosing one of these epistemological positions will lead you to employ a *different* methodology than you would if you chose the other. It is also clear how a researcher's onto-logical and epistemological positions can lead to different views of the same social phenomena.

Box 22   The ontological–epistemological relationship

The thing to note at this juncture is the interrelationship between your ontological and your epistemological positions. As Mason clearly notes:

You should be able to connect the answers to these [the epistemo-logical] questions with your answers to the ontological questions, and the two sets of answers should be consistent so that, for example, your epistemology helps you to generate knowledge and explanations about the ontological components of the social world, be they social processes, social actions, discourses, meanings, or whatever, which you have identified as central...the researcher must recognize not only that there is more than one epistemology, but also that they will not all be complementary or equally consistent with their own ontological position. (1998: 13)

▶ **Differing ontological and epistemological views**

The assumptions underlying research are thus both ontological and epistemological. Plato's famous allegory of the cave is instructive for making us aware of the root of ontology and epistemology, for it shows how very different perceptions of what constitutes reality can exist. Prisoners in a cave are chained in such a way that they can only see forwards, to a wall upon which shadows of artefacts, carried by people behind them, are reflected in the light of a fire.

The prisoners give names and characteristics to these objects which, to them, represent reality. Plato then imagines a scene in which one prisoner leaves the dark cave and sees that not only are the shadows reflections of objects, but also that the objects are depictions of reality. In the text, Socrates says, in conversation with Glaucon:

> Suppose someone tells him [the prisoner released from the cave] that what he's been seeing all this time has no substance, and that he's now closer to reality and is seeing more accurately, because of the greater reality of the things in front of his eyes – what do you imagine his reaction would be? And what do you think he'd say if he were shown any of the passing objects and had to respond to being asked what it was? Don't you think he'd be bewildered and would think that there was more reality in what he'd been seeing before than in what he was being shown now? (Plato 1994: 241–2)

The passage cited above mirrors how some people can come to think in certain ways which are bound by certain cultural and social norms and parameters, for example those established by disciplines in academia. Any premises built upon the experience of the cave-dwellers are certain to differ from those of people on the outside. It is for this reason that we need to be aware of, and understand, that *different* views of the world and *different* ways of gathering knowledge exist. The order in which I have discussed the two terms in this chapter is important, for 'ontology logically precedes epistemology which logically precedes methodology' (i.e. how we go about acquiring the knowledge which exists) (Hay 2002: 63). Interestingly, many research-methods books either discuss these terms the other way around (which, to me, is illogical) or avoid explaining them altogether (which makes it difficult to understand the rest of the book). I should like to take the argument about the interrelationship of the key research components one step further by suggesting that methodology logically precedes research methods which logically precede data sources.

▶ The directional relationship between ontology, epistemology, methodology, methods and sources

It may at first seem somewhat mechanistic and rigid to suggest a directional relationship between the key building blocks of research, but for the purpose of clarity this simplified overview can help demystify an often impenetrable discussion. It is of paramount importance that students understand how a particular view of the world affects the whole research process. By setting out clearly the interrelationship between what a researcher thinks can be researched (her ontological position), linking it to what we can know about it (her epistemological position) and how to go about acquiring it (her methodological approach), you can begin to comprehend the impact your ontological position can have on what and how you decide to study. Ontology is often wrongly collapsed together with epistemology, with the former seen as simply a part of the latter. Whilst the two are closely related, they need to be kept separate, for all research necessarily starts from a person's view of the world, which itself is shaped by the experiences she brings to the research process. As I suggest in chapter 2, a researcher's methodological approach, underpinned by and reflecting specific ontological and epistemological assumptions, represents a *choice* of approach and research methods adopted in a given study.

The method(s) chosen for a research project are inextricably linked to the research questions posed and to the sources of data collected. Figure 1 shows the interrelationship between the building blocks of research.

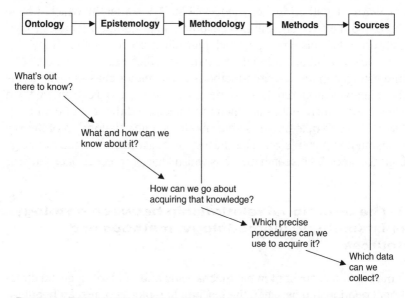

FIGURE 1 THE INTERRELATIONSHIP BETWEEN THE BUILDING BLOCKS OF RESEARCH

Figure 1 may come across as somewhat prescriptive or it may remind readers 'of old style methods books of the 1950s', as one reviewer kindly pointed out. However, I decline to change the figure for the following reasons: the figure shows the directional, and logical, relationship between the key components of research. What the figure *doesn't show* is the impact and influence of the questions one is asking, and the *type* of project one is undertaking, on the methods chosen. However, it is our ontological and epistemological positions that shape the very questions we may ask in the first place, how we pose them and how we set about answering them (see also Devine and Heath 1999: 204). It is possible to agree with the opinion (although I am reluctant) that research may begin at any of the stages in the figure above. For example, a researcher can first choose a favourite or familiar method and then work back through her methodology, epistemology and ontology, *if the researcher makes very sure that the components of research are logically compatible with one another* (see Crotty 1998: 12–14, who advocates starting at either end), although, as I pointed out in chapter 3, research ought to be animated and led by the research questions posed or hypotheses put forward.

Box 23 Taking a different direction?

Now, a reader who has chanced upon some secret documents in the archive of a disgraced dictatorship may doubt the directional relationship advocated above. After all, she would say, 'I'm beginning with rich empirical sources and this has little or nothing to do with ontology, epistemology, methodology and methods, so let me get on with my research.' That would be fair enough, except that a number of observations about the sources – and hence her starting point – need to be made:

1   She would probably hold that the information in the documents in some way represents 'reality' in the former regime and is useful for gaining knowledge about that regime (i.e. this is an ontological and epistemological issue).

2   Our reader's idea of research must be premised on the assumption that documents, written by officials in a discraced dictatorship, are worthy of study (i.e. this is an epistemological issue about knowledge-gathering).

3   In her justification of the use of such documents, their potential and limitations and how they fit within her research strategy, our reader would be engaged in outlining the project's methodology.

Continued

4   She must further subscribe to the view that the method of archival retrieval is bona fide (i.e. the methods).
5   The data produced by archival retrieval, in this case documents on popular opinion, lead to the sources with which our reader began, namely archival documents.

I think, in particular, we should guard against 'method-led' research; that is, allowing ourselves to be led by a particular research method rather than 'question-led' research, whereby research questions point to the most appropriate research method and hence sources. Choosing a research method before having a research question goes against the *logic* of interconnectedness discussed above and will more than likely result in a poor question–method fit. Remember, as I suggested in chapter 2, methods ought to be seen as *free from ontological and epistemological assumptions*, and the choice of which to use should be guided by research questions.

It is important to remember that figure 1 is intended to show the directional relationship between key components of research. However, this does not mean that one component *determines* the other; for example, choosing an ontological position close to that favoured by positivism does not mean your epistemological position will automatically be positivist (see Marsh and Furlong 2002: 17–41). I shall return to this below.

Box 24   The directional relationship in action

Pepper D. Culpepper offers a good example of the effects of a researcher's ontological position on how our research proceeds:

For purposes of explaining the empirical success or failure of cooperation and the formation of common knowledge, there are several key differences between these two approaches (that is, 'rationalists' and 'constructivists'). The first is ontological: rationalists start from the presumption of individualism, whereas constructivists start from a holist ontology. This point of departure leads to a methodological divergence over the preferred unit of analysis. Rationalists show how individual units (say, companies) have defined preferences.... For constructivists... individual understandings of preference are jointly constructed, so the operative unit of analysis is often the network of linked actors. (2003: 10–11)

In order to clarify further some of the points made above, I should like to introduce the so-called 'social capital' debate, which lends itself particularly well to illustrating the importance and impact of ontological and epistemological positions on research. The dominant 'paradigm' in this debate is, to some extent, a good example of method-led research. Scholars have focused primarily on using the research methods inherent in wide-scale surveys to capture such difficult concepts as interpersonal trust and cooperation.

▶ The 'social capital' debate

Broadly speaking, the concept of social capital has come to refer to the by-product of trust relations between people, especially within organisations and associations, in which compromise, debate and face-to-face relations inculcate members with principles of democracy. Active involvement and interest in civic affairs by citizens in a particular region generates a collective good that facilitates collaborative action for all. It is through networks of civic engagement that information flows and is able to be accessed by others. It is the supposed link between the existence of social capital in a specific region and the positive effect this has on governmental and economic performance – and ultimately on democratic governance – that has caught the eye of researchers and policy-makers alike. Generally speaking, the higher the stocks of social capital in society, the more democratic that society is likely to be (Grix 2001b: 189).

The first, and by far the most dominant paradigm in social capital research, the 'Putnam School', consists of a group of scholars who seek to employ Robert Putnam's definition of social capital and, more importantly, though to different degrees, emulate the quantitative research methods employed by Putnam to 'measure' the concept in his study of democracy in Italy (for example, see Hall 1999; Whiteley 1999; Stolle and Rochon 1999). This research paradigm has advanced our thinking on the concept of social capital, but has done so in keeping with the ontological and epistemological underpinnings of Putnam's own work. This paradigm also includes a growing body of work in which the term 'social capital', as used by Putnam, is frequently 'adopted indiscriminately, adapted uncritically, and applied imprecisely' (Woolcock 1998: 196). The original definitions, indicators, methods and methodology used and put forward by these authors are often taken on, regardless of the changes in society and global governance that may have occurred since Putnam's works were written, and regardless of the refinements he has made in his subsequent research (Putnam 1996: 2000).

Putnam and his followers subscribe to similar ontological, epistemological and methodological premises as the fathers of political culture research, Gabriel Almond and Sidney Verba, whose path-breaking work first appeared in the 1950s. Culture, and, in the example here, social capital, is thus seen as something psychological that can be measured at the individual level in a positivist manner through the concrete and quantifiable answers to survey questions (McFalls 2001: p. 2). The vast majority of research on social capital uses survey questions that were *not designed* for capturing indicators of what is thought to make up social capital (an excellent exception to this general rule is Richard Rose's social-capital survey discussed in Rose 1999). Rather, answers to questions designed for other purposes are drawn on to prove the existence or demise of trust and co-operation and thus social capital in society.

The 'Putnam School' of social-capital research can be said to be based on a foundationalist *ontology* (i.e. they believe the world exists independently of our knowledge of it) and a positivist *epistemology*. This starting point leads to the favoured *methodology* of this group. This broad term entails the reflections on the potentialities and limitations of particular techniques or research methods. Importantly, methodology constitutes a *choice* of research strategy which, for the 'Putnam School', is quantitative, involving a large number of cases. This choice leads them to adopt a particular research *method*, the questionnaire, from which the respondents' answers to questions are aggregated and manipulated statistically. Thus, a quantitative measure of cognitive responses to survey questions (the *data sources*) is used as an index to decide whether social capital is in decline or not. It is not difficult to see how the starting point for researchers (ontology) is crucially linked to the other building blocks of research. To reiterate the above example, a foundationalist ontology (i.e. one based on an 'unquestionable set of indisputable beliefs from which our knowledge may be logically deduced; Hughes and Sharrock 1997: 4–5) generally leads to a positivist epistemology (i.e. one which focuses on observable and measurable social phenomena). It is important to remain aware, however, that researchers may begin with a foundationalist ontology and then proceed to a realist epistemology, which differs greatly from a positivist epistemology (see chapter 5). These initial positions lead to a methodology that chooses quantitative research strategies over qualitative and points the researcher to the specific method of measuring a response to a survey. Ironically, perhaps, in the above example scholars adopting a foundationalist ontology, which would usually mean that they believe that social phenomena must be directly observable, are studying something that cannot itself be clearly observed: trust. The concept of trust, which is central to an understanding of social capital, has a strong normative content, something that a positivist epistemology is not well suited to unpacking.

If, however, you do not conceive of social capital as the sum total of cognitive responses to questions of trust, but rather as something that is affected by, and adheres to, social structures, your research design would look quite different. I could argue, for example, that the social context in which the networks of relations between people are embedded is essential to the analysis. Thus, as Maloney et al. (2000: 16) suggest, drawing heavily on Coleman (1988), social capital 'should be understood as context dependent, and as a resource that inheres in the relations between actors'. The wider factors that shape and inform local social contexts are surely related to a country's mode of governance? Whether a particular mode of governance is more conducive to the creation or existence of social capital than another is rarely discussed by the 'Putnam School' because of their ontological and epistemological position. Governance can range, for example, from centralist to federalist or liberal democratic to authoritarian. Does a decentralised form of governance translate into politics closer to the people? Is it more sensitive towards, and committed to, local causes? Does it foster greater participation of citizens in the political process, thereby creating ties between community groups and local governments?

Let us look at a different research strategy that starts from a different ontological and epistemological position: let's say I believe that institutional structures and modes of governance matter for the existence, maintenance and creation of social capital. Such an approach lays emphasis on the 'conditions of action', the structure that either facilitates or constrains action (Sibeon 1999: 142). Analysing social capital as a dependent variable (as opposed to an independent variable as most social capital researchers do), one affected profoundly by the type of governance in a given country and its specific set of political structures and institutions, allows for an understanding of different social contexts within which interaction and relations between actors and institutions are carried out. Interestingly, asking people directly how they experience their own relations both within and between specific groups can lead to very different results from those of the 'Putnam School' above. For example, in a small pilot project focusing on the ability of 'Euroregions' to foster trust and social capital between bordering countries (Germany and Poland), the following results were found (Grix and Knowles 2003). First, after in-depth interviews with both sides of the Euroregion, it emerged that one of the biggest hindrances to the development of 'between-group' social capital was in fact the lack of 'within-group' social capital among actors keen to promote cross-border co-operation on the respective sides of the border. Thus a different research strategy was able to unravel the lack of opportunity structures through which information could be shared and personal, face-to-face interaction could take place. In this way it was possible to gain an overview of the structures that existed to promote or hinder co-operation and understand the actors' perception of these structures, including their assessment of their access to specific information channels. As we have seen, this type of analysis, sometimes termed the 'double hermeneutic' (see chapter 5 for an explanation of this), is not acceptable to our full-blown positivist mentioned earlier; she would use different methods to get at such information or she would not consider an actor's perception of her situation of as much relevance or importance as, say, cross-border economic flows between the countries.

This type of 'interpretivist' approach, which emphasises the role of both agents and structures, is the opposite of the agent-centred approach outlined above. The ontological position differs from the 'Putnam School' and can be termed 'anti-foundationalist' (i.e. not all social phenomena are directly observable; structures exist that cannot be observed and those that can may not present the social and political world as it actually is; see Marsh and Smith 2001: 530). This then affects my epistemological position (i.e. the extent to which I believe we can know about social capital in a specific context and the extent to which we can generalise beyond it) and of course my methodology (i.e. the research strategy chosen to acquire this knowledge). Within this methodology I have chosen the precise procedures or research methods to get at **empirical** questions which have been affected by my ontological and epistemological positions (within the real project, in-depth élite interviews were complemented by a documentary analysis and guided by a theoretical approach).

Table 1 summarises the differences in the two approaches I have outlined. Both approaches may, for example, choose similar research methods to undertake the research, but they would lay emphasis on *different* methods and sources and would analyse the data differently, depending on their ontological and epistemological positions. For example, the 'alternative approach' may well use quantitative data to gain an understanding

TABLE 1 ALTERNATIVE APPROACHES TO SOCIAL CAPITAL RESEARCH

Approach	Ontology	Epistemology	Methodology	Methods	Sources
'Putnam School'	Foundationalist	Positivist	Choice of quantitative strategy, using multiple cases and surveys	Questionnaire via wide-scale survey	Answers to questions in questionnaire
Alternative approach	Anti-foundationalist	Interpretivist	Choice of both quantitative and qualitative strategy, usually using small number of in-depth cases.	In-depth interviews; documentary analysis	Interview transcripts and background statistical data

of the volume of trade across the border between Germany and Poland, but the researcher writing within this research paradigm would not necessarily make inferences or generalisations from this data.

The implications for research and policy of such an interconnectedness of the building blocks of research are obvious. In America, for example, the term social capital – as propounded by Putnam et al. – has been 'borrowed' by idealists on the ideological right in a debate about de Tocqueville's America, involving a return to the morals and the 'good' society of that era, for this ideal is equated with a reduction in crime and a return to a sense of civic responsibility. If, however, the assumptions upon which this type of approach is based are shown to be shaky, a question mark remains over their final conclusions.

Finally, it is worth emphasising that it is unimportant whether you agree with the arguments put forward in the social-capital debate outlined above. The point is to see how *different* starting points of research lead to *different* research strategies. It is precisely for this reason that we need to understand the 'footings' of research.

▶ Summary

In order to produce good, clear scholarship, you need to understand fully the language with which you are working. There is no better place to start than with the building blocks of research: ontology, epistemology, methodology, methods and sources. Some researchers may consider the key terms discussed above and the need to understand ontology and epistemology, in particular, as separate from practical, on-the-ground research. This is wrong on several accounts and the main points of this chapter sum up why this is the case:

- You need to understand the logic behind the approaches taken by others and you need to make your own approach very clear, whatever research you do.
- This will allow you to defend your own positions, understand other researchers' positions and fully grasp the directional relationship of key components of the research process.
- It will allow you to engage properly in academic debate.
- It will assist you in producing quality and transparent research projects.

▶ Essential reading

Bryman, A. (2001) *Social Research Methods*, Oxford, Oxford University Press, chapter 1.

Hay, C. (2002) *Political Analysis*, Basingstoke, Palgrave Macmillan, chapter 2.

Marsh, D. and Furlong, P. (2002) 'A Skin not a Sweater: Ontology and Epistemology in Political Science', in D. Marsh and G. Stoker (eds), *Theory and Methods in Political Science*, Basingstoke, Palgrave Macmillan, updated and revised edn, chapter 1.

Mason, J. (1998) *Qualitative Researching*, London, Thousand Oaks CA, and New Delhi, Sage, chapter 2.

5 Introducing the Key Research Paradigms

Chapter 5 introduces:

- *Three key research paradigms: positivism, post-positivism (critical realism) and interpretivism*
- *A brief overview of post-modernism and feminism*
- *A discussion of the key perspectives in economics, political science, international relations, sociology and history*
- *A brief discussion of disciplines and interdisciplinarity*

This chapter provides a broad overview of the key tenets in the traditions of research and the key perspectives in core academic disciplines in the human sciences that derive directly from them. It is by no means exhaustive, but is limited to the main research paradigms and a selective discussion of central **perspectives** in the following disciplines: economics, political science, international relations, sociology and history

The purpose of expounding on the research traditions in the human sciences is to equip you with enough knowledge of the language used and issues raised in discussions on the roots of research to enable you confidently to read and orientate yourself through the material pertaining to your research. The following *is not* intended to replace an in-depth discussion of the philosophy of research. Under the broad headings I use below, many 'families' of research strands are gathered and although there are qualitative differences between such strands, it aids understanding if we know that they are linked to cognate areas.

A great number of research books on the market skip this section altogether, or they divide the traditions of research into two, neat, opposing paradigms (see, for example, Denscombe 2002): positivism (usually building upon the so-called 'scientific method') and interpretivism. By adding a third research paradigm, I am following other researchers (Marsh and Furlong 2002; Guba and Lincoln 1998; Robson 2002) in offering you a broad overview of the research paradigms you are likely to encounter in the human sciences. This overview will help 'place' the main academic perspectives – discussed in the second half of the chapter – according to the research paradigms within which they operate. Such a broad presentation of the -isms of the human sciences has a number of benefits:

- It allows us to understand the intellectual foundations of the core perspectives in the mainstream human-science disciplines.
- It helps us to see how close many of the perspectives in different academic disciplines actually are.
- Finally, such an undertaking familiarises us with the language, terms, limitations, potential, key components and core texts associated with the main perspectives we are likely to encounter.

Such a broad-brush approach also has a number of disadvantages – for example, what about the perspectives I do not mention? Also, many proponents of the research paradigms and perspectives outlined below would argue for a more differentiated or even a completely different categorisation. Nonetheless, I believe the advantages of this exercise outweigh the disadvantages. What this discussion does do is to introduce you to many of the most important terms you are likely to meet throughout your studies. It is useful to know the difference between say 'positivism' and 'realism' in international relations. The former should be used for broad categories of research, as I have done here; the latter refers to a specific perspective, which draws on many of the assumptions found under positivist research.

I should like to make it clear that the following discussion, although based on traditional academic disciplines, in no way attempts to uphold the often rigid boundaries between the disciplines I am outlining. In fact, a further aim of this chapter is to encourage you to look beyond your own discipline by showing that disciplinary perspectives draw from wider roots which are common to many of them. A final section of this chapter deals exclusively with the notions of disciplines and interdisciplinarity.

I commence with a brief outline of the key research paradigms, which consists of boiling them down to ten core premises. While this involves oversimplification, I believe it will be enough for students to locate their projects amidst the bewildering array of -isms frequently used in academia. I then turn to the key perspectives in the human sciences within these research paradigms. I offer an initial graphic overview of the perspectives aligned within their respective paradigmatic research traditions. The pattern of the subsequent discussion and presentation of the perspectives closely follows Colin Hay's exposition of key perspectives in political science and international relations (see 2002: 6–28). By way of demonstration, I outline the assumptions, key themes, key concepts, limitations, chief advocates and 'must' reads (that is, the seminal works associated with them) of a selection of the 15 perspectives highlighted. My purpose is not to give you a blow-by-blow account of each and every perspective, but rather to indicate the way in which academic perspectives from different disciplines are linked by their philosophical roots.

▶ Research paradigms

Any form of categorisation is likely to be imprecise and leave out more than it contains. Yet research paradigms, that is, our understanding of *what* one can know about something and *how* one can gather knowledge about it, are inherent in every single approach to the study of society. Generally, in the philosophy of the social and human sciences, there are three broad paradigms: the positivist, post-positivist and interpretivist positions (an 'interpretivist' position is *also* post-positivist; however, as I seek to make clear below, this particular paradigm acts as an umbrella term for specific approaches to social enquiry). As we shall see, these positions are often labelled differently, which makes the discourse on this topic confusing. Below I set out the three positions on a continuum: as we move from left to right (from positivist to interpretivist positions), we go from approaches attempting to 'explain' social reality to those seeking to 'interpret' or 'understand' it:

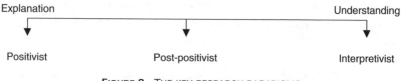

Explanation

Understanding

Positivist

Post-positivist

Interpretivist

FIGURE 2 THE KEY RESEARCH PARADIGMS

As I suggested above, these categories are broad and often overlap; for example, interpretivism is post-positivist, but it is a distinct paradigm linked to understanding in research. Also, the clear distinction between 'explanation' and 'understanding' should only be taken as a guide, as many interpretivists seek to explain and positivists would hope their analyses help us understand social phenomena. Why is it important to understand the core paradigms in research? According to Clough and Nutbrown, who advised us in chapter 4 *not* to elaborate on the assumptions underpinning our research, such research paradigms, or meta-theories, are '*post hoc* frameworks for characterising the means and concerns of a given study.... Hence the idea of choice *between* broad approaches characterised in this way is ultimately spurious' (2002: 15). This is seemingly difficult to square with the view, which I share, that 'Metatheory should ... be a central feature in all planning of social science study, and should not be introduced *ad hoc*, since there is otherwise a great risk of the work being conducted in an unsystematic and inconsequent manner. In other words there should always be a clear connection between the ontological and epistemological starting points and the practical research work' (Danermark et al. 2002, 4). This echoes the view I put forward in chapter 4: our starting point affects the rest of the whole research process. For this reason, the following briefly outlines the central tenets of the core research paradigms and highlights other names and varieties by which they may be known.

The core of positivism

Positivism – and those research perspectives I have associated with it – has proved to be the most dominant research paradigm of the past century. This, and the fact that more recent paradigms use it as a marker against which they seek to differentiate themselves, has led to a wealth of literature on this subject. For this reason, the following section is slightly longer than the subsequent descriptions of other paradigms.

Box 25   Positivism: A broad church

According to Hughes and Sharrock (1997: 24) whose words serve as an introduction to this section, we need to be cautious when using the term positivism:

The critics of positivist social science.... Like all critics have a tendency to present a picture of the opposition, in this case positivism, as if it were not only stupid but without any subtlety and variety. Although it is necessary to give a summary, hence simplified, picture of positivism, the reader is warned that it is neither a stupid position, though it might

Continued

---

be wrong, nor a monolithic school of thought. What we here refer to as 'positivism' includes or overlaps with positions which identify themselves by other names – 'empiricism', 'behaviourism', 'naturalism' – and some which even identify themselves as *the* scientific approach. Just to make things complicated, some of these same names are sometimes used to identify antipositivist positions.

Martin Hollis complements this with the following:

Positivism is a term with many uses in social science and philosophy. At the broad end, it embraces any approach which applies scientific method to human affairs conceived as belonging to a natural order open to objective enquiry. (1999: 41)

Positivism – which, technically speaking, is an epistemological approach (see chapter 4) – is a very broad term under which many different approaches to social enquiry are known. Its historical legacy is said to stretch back to Aristotle and has been developed, in a variety of ways, by such figures as Francis Bacon, René Descartes, Auguste Comte, Thomas Hobbes, David Hume, John Stuart Mill and Émile Durkheim (Hughes and Sharrock 1997: 25–7; see chapter 6 of this volume for Durkheim's middle-range theory of suicide). Many of these key figures looked upon natural science as a model for the human sciences, in the process seeking to unearth a unitary methodology of the social and natural sciences.

Other terms related to this broad rubric include empiricism, objectivism, the 'scientific method' – by which positivism is clearly influenced – naturalism and a 'naturalist approach' (Marsh and Furlong 2002: 18). Although there are significant qualitative differences between all of these ontological positions and disciplinary perspectives, they tend to subscribe to the broad principles below. Positivism itself, it must be said, is a very broad church, so the following should be taken only as a rough guide.

Instead of going into minute detail about the differences between the approaches usually listed under the umbrella term 'positivism', I have limited myself to what I believe to be the ten most significant premises on which this paradigm is based:

1 Positivism is based on a realist, foundationalist ontology (Guba and Lincoln 1998: 204), which views the world as existing independently of our knowledge of it.

2   Positivists believe that 'There are patterns and regularities, causes and consequences, in the social world just as there are in the natural world' (Denscombe 2002: 14). A positivist position believes in the possibility of making causal statements.

3   Therefore, many seek to employ scientific methods to analyse the social world.

4   These methods are neutral, as are the researchers using them. Thus they do not disturb what exists (ibid., 15).

5   Positivists lay great emphasis on explanation in social research, as opposed to understanding, and many believe that the 'real purpose of explanation is prediction' (Rubinstein 1981: 11).

6   This group emphasises the observational and verificational dimensions of *empirical* practice (reality can be 'captured' by our senses), whilst making a clear distinction between 'fact' and 'value': positivists are more concerned with the former and less with the latter (Hughes and Sharrock 1997: 28).

7   Positivists show 'an aversion to metaphysics as having any rightful place in philosophical inquiry proper' (ibid.).

8   Positivists seek 'objectivity' in research (Marsh and Furlong 2002: 18).

9   A researcher in the positivist tradition believes that we can establish regular relationships between social phenomena by using theory to generate hypotheses, which can then be tested by direct observation.

10 Finally, positivists do not recognise what Anthony Giddens has termed 'the double hermeneutic'. This term refers to the act of interpreting an actor's perception or interpretation (Interpretation 1) of his or her situation in a particular context (Interpretation 2): effectively an interpretation of an interpretation (Hollis 1999: 146).

Most positivists assume there is no dichotomy between what we see (appearance) and how things really are ('reality') and that the world is real and neither mediated by our senses nor socially constructed (in contrast to realism and interpretivism below; see Marsh and Furlong 2002: 26–30). Furthermore, the belief in causal statements is shared by realism but contrasts with interpretivism. Positivism places an emphasis on empirical theory in the production of knowledge; it rejects normative questions (i.e. question of values, trust, etc.) and believes that social science can be value-free (i.e. it believes in the value-neutrality of researchers when investigating the social world).

   The attractiveness of an approach seeking the precision, exactitude and power of prediction promised by the natural sciences is understandable. The human sciences can be messy, people unpredictable and factors leading to events hard to unravel. Positivism attempts to overcome this messiness by seeking rules and laws with which to render the social world understandable.

The core of interpretivism

Interpretivism is an umbrella term which covers just as many variations of approach to social enquiry as positivism above. Under this very broad heading we can gather a wide range of positions, for example relativism, *Verstehen* ('understanding' – usually associated with the work of Max Weber [see Outhwaite 1986], and the opposite to 'explanation', although Weber's 'explanatory understanding' renders the classification 'interpretivism' for his body of work difficult), phenomonology, hermeneutics, idealism (the philosophical doctrine), symbolic interactionism and constructionism, to name but a few (see also Neuman 2000: 70–5; Blaikie 2000: 114). The key influences cited in relation to this paradigm include the influential German thinkers Immanuel Kant, G. W. Hegel, Max Weber, Wilhelm Dilthey and Hans Georg Gadamer; American sociologists, George Herbert Mead, Ervin Goffman and, more recently, Barney Glaser and Anselm Strauss. Again, there are qualitative differences between all of these approaches, but they have several things in common, the first of which is an *anti-positivist* position.

Box 26   What's interpretivism?

As with the other two research paradigms outlined here, interpretivism is an umbrella term which covers a very wide range of perspectives in the human sciences. One can, however, note some general features of this paradigm in order to give you an idea of what it is supposed to mean. Amongst other things, interpretivism can be looked upon in part as a response to the over-dominance of positivism. The reason why so many authors choose to outline positivism and interpretivism – and thereby leave out a whole host of social research between these binary poles – is because they can be seen as opposites: positivists seek objectivity while interpretivists believe in subjectivity; positivists tend to model their research on the natural sciences while interpretivists believe there is a clear distinction to be made between the natural and the social world, and therefore we need a methodology and methods of gathering data that are more in tune with the subjects we are studying.

An important point to note is that while the demarcations between research paradigms are not as clear-cut as I have set out, and while the best research is often undertaken on the margins of two research paradigms, you *cannot* combine an approach which draws on both positivist and interpretivist paradigms, as the fundamental assumptions underlying the paradigms are logically incompatible. Denscombe (2002: 21–2) outlines the type of research expected under this heading:

> The interpretivists' concern with 'subjectivity', with 'understandings', with 'agency' and the way people construct their social world, introduces complexities that involve elements of uncertainty. There is even the possibility of contradictions and internal inconsistencies arising as part of the explanations that interpretivists produce. This does not sit comfortably with the scientific search for universal laws or certainty about how things work. To caricature things a little, interpretivists' explanations are likely to be messy rather than nice and neat. They might be open-ended rather than complete.

A number of core premises of the interpretivist paradigm can be identified. Once again, I have limited the discussion to ten points, although other commentators would undoubtedly mention a number of different premises:

1 Interpretivist positions, in contrast to positivism and realism, are based on an anti-foundationalist ontology (see chapter 4, p. 57), and subscribe to the view that the world does not exist independently of our knowledge of it.
2 The world is socially constructed through the interaction of individuals and the separation of 'fact' and 'value' is not so clear-cut as the positivists claim.
3 The emphasis in this paradigm is on understanding as opposed to explanation, as interpretivists do not believe in relying on mere observation for understanding social phenomena.
4 In contrast to positivism, this position sees the social and natural sciences as being distinct from one another. With this in mind, the social world needs to be studied from within and with methods different from those used in the study of the natural sciences.
5 Social phenomena do not exist independently of our interpretation of them and it is these interpretations which affect outcomes. Thus researchers are inextricably part of the social reality being researched, i.e. they are not 'detached' from the subject they are studying.

6 Therefore, 'objective' – or value-free – analysis is impossible, because knowledge is theoretically and discursively laden and a researcher necessarily is the sum total of his or her own personal – and subjective – opinions, attitudes and values.
7 Interpretivists acknowledge the 'double hermeneutic' as a means of understanding society, social actors and *their* perceptions of *their* role or position in society.
8 Interpretivists, in general, do not strive to establish causal explanations in the social world, as their emphasis is on understanding (note that Max Weber *did* believe in constructing causal explanations).
9 Researchers in this paradigm tend to place emphasis on meaning in the study of social life and emphasise the role language plays in constructing 'reality'.
10 In particular, they stress the meanings given to the world in which those studied live (Williams and May 2000: 59–63).

Now that I have discussed the two ends of our continuum, let us turn to the paradigm which comes between both: critical realism.

The core of post-positivism – critical realism

As our continuum (figure 2) shows, post-positivism can be understood as a research paradigm placed between both positivism and interpretivism. A note on this term is in order before we start. Many textbooks choose the term 'realism' to describe the paradigm between positivism and interpretivism. Whilst the division of paradigms is necessary and admirable, the term 'realism' is somewhat confusing, as it represents an *ontological* position which is shared in part by positivism and a number of perspectives under the label 'post-positivism'. Positivism and parts of post-positivism share a realist, foundationalist ontology, but positivism tends towards empirical realism – i.e. it treats the world as consisting of observable objects, a world with no unobservable qualities (Sayer 2000: 11) – and the post-positivist account we are interested in here tends towards a *critical realism*. One way of conceiving of critical realism as I use the term here, attributed to the thinking of the philosopher Roy Bhaskar, is to think of it as a broad research paradigm, which is related to a variety of approaches under the heading of a 'critical social science'. There are a great number of 'realisms' (e.g. 'scientific realism', 'transcendental realism', see Robson 2002: 29) all drawing from the basic tenets of realism, but I shall opt for the term 'critical realism' in the following passages, as this appears to be the most influential strand of realism in the human sciences.

Most commentators trace the historical antecedents of this approach back to the work of Karl Marx, Sigmund Freud, Theodor Adorno and Herbert Marcuse. This paradigm has also been influenced by the Frankfurt School in Germany (see Neuman 2000: 75–81).

Critical realism
Since the 1970s, a powerful alternative to both positivism, with its search for regular laws, and interpretivism, with its emphasis on 'the interpretation of meaning' (Sayer 2000: 2–3), has grown in importance. Put simply, critical-realist scholars have attempted to combine the 'how' (understanding – which is linked to interpretivism) and the 'why' (explanation – which is linked to positivism) approaches by bridging the gap between the two extremes (see May 2001: 15–16).

Box 27   Getting to the bottom of (critical) 'realism'

Peter Kerr succinctly summarises the core of (critical) realism when he suggests:

Realism . . . differs from positivism in two important respects. Firstly, realists invoke a much more layered conception of ontology. Realism works on the assumption of 'depth ontology' – i.e. that these generative mechanisms are highly complex, often structural and most crucially, not always directly observable. In this sense, part of the explanatory schema must be an attempt at 'interpreting' causal links from observable outcomes. By not restricting its focus to directly observable causal links, the 'depth ontology' which realism offers is able to produce a much richer layer of explanatory variables and generative mechanisms than rival positivist explanations . . . . Secondly, the incorporation of agency into the explanatory schema means that the analyst must take an even bolder step beyond positivism. Given that agents are themselves active in interpreting their own structural context and that the meanings which they attach to any given situation are likely to differ, part of the quest for explanation must be the incorporation of the notion of hermeneutics; i.e. an understanding of the differential meanings which agents infer upon their actions. (2003: 122–3).

As in the previous two sections, the following offers an outline sketch of some of the important characteristics of critical realism:

1 Critical realism straddles both the positivist and interpretivist para-digms, sharing a foundationalist ontology with positivism and allowing for interpretation in research.
2 A critical-realist approach believes that while social science can use the same methods as natural science regarding causal explanation (in line with positivism), it also needs to move away from them by adopting an interpretive understanding (Sayer 2000: 17).
3 Critical realists, unlike interpretivists, generally seek not only to understand but also to *explain* the social world.
4 Critical realists conceive of social change and conflict in society as not always apparent or observable, believing that 'the immediately perceived characteristics of objects, events, or social relations rarely reveal everything' (Neuman 2000: 77), i.e. we need to look beyond the surface.
5 Furthermore, critical realists believe in a 'structured' or 'stratified' reality which requires a 'depth ontology' and the interpretation of causal links not always observable in order to offer a fuller explan-ation of an event, object, social relations, etc.
6 According to critical realists, 'all human agency occurs and acquires meaning only in relation to already preconstituted, and deeply structured, settings' (Hay 1995: 200). That is, pre-existing structures affect and are affected by actors.
7 Whilst acknowledging that interpretive understanding is an important feature of social science, the objects and structures in society are understood to have *causal* powers, so critical realists are able to make causal statements and identify causal *mechanisms*, in con-trast to interpretivists (Sayer 2000: 6). However, 'realists' idea of causation is different from positivists' (Lewis 2002: 22; Williams and May 2000: 83; see below).
8 Structure and agency are looked upon as mutually constitutive, but they can be treated as separate for analytical purposes, thereby facilitating research (Hay 2002: 127; Archer et al. 1998: 203).
9 Crucially, critical realism is compatible with a wide range of research methods and suggests that the choice of which method to employ should depend on the nature of the object of study and what we want to learn about it (Sayer 2000: 19).
10 Finally, many critical realists, unlike positivists, acknowledge the double hermeneutic.

Importantly, a critical realist's belief in 'causes' is not as clear-cut as a positivist's: causes do not simply *determine* action; instead 'what causes something to happen has nothing to do with the number of times we have observed it happening. Explanation depends rather on identifying causal mechanisms and how they work, and discovering if they have been activated and under what conditions' (Sayer 2000: 14). Critical realists tend to distinguish between *efficient causes* (actors) and *material causes* (social structures), suggesting that both represent causal forces: the first by initiating action and the second by constraining or facilitating such action (for an excellent account, see Lewis 2002: 17–23).

Summary of research paradigms

The three core research paradigms above are the headings under which I shall introduce the key perspectives in research. As I have suggested, these are broad-brush terms that do, however, capture most of the significant features of the key paradigms in research. Before introducing the disciplinary perspectives that operate within these paradigms, it is worth looking briefly at two particular research perspectives that have gained in significance in the recent past: post-modernism and feminism. It is difficult to categorise these two -isms (they are neither 'disciplines' nor 'research paradigms'), but the broad term 'emancipatory' seems to capture what is generally understood under these headings. Box 28 seeks to give you a flavour of post-modernism and feminism; what it does not do is tell you how deeply influential – and controversial – these perspectives have been. Both have questioned the very assumptions upon which most 'mainstream' research is based. They represent not just different applications of theory to research practice, but they also put many of the accepted norms and fundamentals of research in question. This, in turn, has led to a great deal of methodological reflection, justification and clarification, which, if not taken too far, can be good for research as a whole.

Box 28 What are post-modernism and feminism? 'Emancipatory' perspectives

Post-modernism is *an ontological position* which views 'traditional' knowledge claims (i.e. epistemological positions) with scepticism. In many disciplines, it does not have specific perspectives, but is simply

Continued

known as a 'post-modern' approach or 'post-modernism'. The most well-known perspectives associated with post-modernism are 'deconstructivism' (associated with Derrida), the 'genealogical approach' (associated with Foucault) and 'discourse analysis' (this latter is a research method used by most research paradigms).

Post-modernism by its very nature defies definition, but an attempt at capturing at least some of its characteristics is as follows:

Postmodernism reflects a decline of absolutes – no longer does following the correct method guarantee true results. Instead of only one truth and one certainty, we are more ready to accept that there are many truths and that the only certainty is uncertainty ... the orthodox consensus about how to do research scientifically has been displaced. As we have seen, there are many research traditions each with its own epistemology. Postmodernism, however, is not an alternative tradition, although it does foreground the epistemological commitments which are implicit in all research traditions.

To do research in a post-modern way is to take a critical stance towards the practice of sense-making and sense-taking which we call research. (Usher et al. 1997: 210–11, cited in Punch 2000a: 147–8)

Much feminist work is based on an anti-foundationalist ontological position which challenges the androcentric (male-centred) nature of research in general (though by no means all). Like post-modernism, feminism does not favour any particular research method – although there is a tendency towards qualitative research, above all because feminist researchers do not believe in value-free or 'objective' research. Rather, many celebrate the 'personal' in research, advocating that the researcher actively seeks to mobilise *her* past experiences when researching others. For example, Sasha Roseneil suggests, towards the end of her study of women at Greenham Common: 'I can but advocate that more sociologists look to their own unique life-histories and experiences for inspiration of their research' (1993: 205, cited in Devine and Heath 1999: 196).

Within feminism there are a number of different 'strands', ranging from empirical feminists to 'standpoint' feminists (see May 2001: 17–26 for an overview of these approaches).

To confuse matters, feminists can also use a post-modern approach (scholars in this group tend to be 'feminist relativists') and, indeed, both share many of the same concerns. Feminist post-modernism tends to 'reject the epistemological assumptions of modernist, Enlightenment thought. Thus, it stands opposed to the foundationalist grounding of knowledge, the universalizing claims for the scope of knowledge, and the employment of dualistic categories of thought. By contrast, postmodern feminism is an epistemology that is non-foundationalist, contextualist, and nondualist, or multiplist, in its commitments' (Haig 1997: 182, cited in Punch 2000a: 142).

▶ Key perspectives in research

As I pointed out in the introduction and reiterate below, the following form of categorisation is a simplification of how academics see their and others' perspectives in the human sciences. The alternative to attempting to bring some order to the wide variety of overlapping perspectives is to leave discussion of them to individual disciplines. I do not support this view, given that much excellent work is carried out which cannot be pigeonholed in one or other discipline. The complexities of modern-day life, in which politics and economics are inextricably entwined, where understanding history is essential for understanding the present, and a knowledge of a single academic discipline may not be enough to understand or 'capture' social processes at work, make looking beyond narrow disciplinary boundaries an essential item in every student's knapsack.

The following overview proceeds by summarising the perspectives we are going to discuss in Table 2. The idea at this stage is to hint at how these perspectives relate to (a) the foundations of research and (b) each other. A number of observations are in order before we introduce a selection of the individual perspectives highlighted above. The first important caveat of this type of characterisation is that the division between research paradigms is nowhere near as precise and clinical as I have presented them here. They are in fact imprecise and often overlapping. As I suggested, much of the best academic work goes on between research paradigms. This is not to contradict what we discussed in chapter 4, when I warned of chopping and changing our ontological and epistemological positions *as and when we please*. But there is nothing logically wrong in combining certain ontological and epistemological positions: for example, a realist epistemology with interpretivism and a positivist epistemology with a realist epistemology. However, you should note that this *does not* hold for positivism and interpretivism, one of the reasons these positions are so often outlined as binary opposites in textbooks.

Table 2 Key disciplinary perspectives (aligned according to research paradigm positions)

Discipline	Positivism	Critical realism	Interpretivism
Economics	Neoclassical economics ('positivist economics')	Marxist economics	Interpretivist economics
Sociology	Functionalism	Critical realist	Symbolic interactionism
History	Empiricist	Critical realist	Life history
Politics	Rational choice theory (but also behaviouralism, rational choice institutionalism)	Critical realist	Sociological institutionalism
International relations	Realism, neorealism and neoliberalism		Reflectivist theories
	← Social constructivism →		

Also, it is worth noting again at this stage that many of the protagonists working within the perspectives above would dispute the terminology used and the positions in which I have placed their perspectives. More significantly, perhaps, many scholars would not agree with the exercise of trying to take a snapshot of an evolving and developing area of research. The perspectives offered below should be seen as *indicative* only and serve to show how different disciplines can draw from (broadly) similar philosophical roots.

Key perspectives in the 'positivist' tradition

To give you a flavour of the manner in which the roots of research bind distinct disciplines, I shall run through those perspectives associated with the positivist paradigm of research in more detail. The points made hold for the two other research paradigms; many disciplinary perspectives share similar assumptions and roots, an insight which, once we are aware of it, aids our understanding of a wide variety of approaches to social phenomena.

The order in which I wish to discuss the perspectives under this heading are as follows:

- neoclassical economics
- rational choice theory
- realism (in IR)
- functionalism
- empiricist history.

The first core perspective is 'neoclassical economics', which shares many of the same core assumptions that underlie rational choice theory (political science and economics), realism (i.e. the international-relations variety), functionalism (sociology) and empiricism (history). Table 3 crudely attempts to capture the key characteristics of this perspective. As we saw in chapter 2, this economic 'paradigm' has been dominant in the UK and US since the 1970s. Interestingly, many of the key assumptions articulated by protagonists such as Milton Friedman have found their way into the study of the international system (see international relations below).

Closest to this economic perspective in terms of assumptions and world-view is perhaps rational choice theory (RCT) in political science,

Table 3 ECONOMICS: NEOCLASSICAL ECONOMICS

Key assumptions:
- Generally focuses on market mechanisms and the allocation of resources made through markets
- Independently minded individuals are free to choose what they want and what action to take, decisions which can be rationalised in terms of aims and means (see Boland 2001: 567)
- State intervention ought to be kept to a minimum or research focuses on the correct level of state intervention
- Positive economics can be 'objective' like any of the physical sciences (Friedman 1953: 4).

Key themes:
- Highlights the role of the 'market' as the key mechanism to allocate resources
- Focused on limiting state intervention in the process of market allocation
- Sees the control of inflation as paramount to the functioning of the market economy

Key concepts:
- Predictive hypotheses
- The market
- Supply and demand; game theory
- Resource allocation and equilibrium

Limitations:
- The neoclassical approach tends to overemphasise the role of agents and play down the role of context
- In the search for scientific rigour, there is a tendency to explain human society using mathematical models

Key advocates and seminal works:
- P. A. Samuelson, *Foundations of Economic Analysis* (1947)
- Alfred Marshall, *Principles of Economics* (1890)
- Milton Friedman, *Essays in Positive Economics* (1953)

and realism in international relations. RCT tends to focus on the individual as the key unit of analysis and shares the notions of rationality and objectivity that are often associated with the neo-classical perspective in economics. It must be said that within RCT there are a wide variety of approaches, ranging from 'hard' to 'soft', with the former attempting to emulate the mathematical calculus of neoclassical economists' analyses and the latter incorporating elements of other perspectives, for example institutionalism. The point is, however, that the general overview presented here reveals the roots of RCT.

The belief in the logic and power of the market held by neoclassical economists is mirrored in RCT by a belief in the utility-maximising potential of the individual, as he or she is guided in life by specific preferences, irrespective of the context in which choices are made. Finally, RCT can be seen as an attempt to 'import the rigour and predictive power of neo-classical economics into political science', whilst also trying to 'model (mathematically) the implications of human rationality for political conduct' (Hay 2002: 8).

Within international relations, the perspective which is most closely aligned to the two already introduced is realism. Hollis and Smith sum up the core of realism and its relation to the positivist paradigm thus:

> The Realist approach . . . gets its name from precisely that point: that it deals with human nature as it is and not as it ought to be, and with historical events as they have occurred, not as they should have occurred. Moreover, the approach was trying to create a *science* of international relations. This made it an essentially *Positivistic* way of analysing events, since it relied on a notion of underlying forces producing behaviour. (Hollis and Smith: 1990. 23, my emphasis)

Such a scientific and positivistic approach retains the 'objectivity' of the perspectives above and emphasises the rationality of states' actions *vis-à-vis* one another.

The next disciplinary perspective under the umbrella of positivism is functionalism, which dominated mainstream sociological and anthropological theory for the best part of the twentieth century, with many of the most well-known sociologists, for example Émile Durkheim, Talcott Parsons and his student Robert Merton, a key figure in developing 'middle-range-theory' – see Chapter 6 – advancing this perspective. Broadly, functionalism sought to uncover the rules that governed the

Table 4 POLITICS: RATIONAL CHOICE THEORY (RCT)

Key assumptions
- Individual actors are the basic unit of analysis
- They are rational, efficient and instrumental utility-maximisers who seek to maximise personal utility
- They have a clear hierarchy of preferences such that in any given context there is only one optimal course of action available to them

Key themes
- The aggregation of individually rational behaviour frequently produces collectively irrational outcomes
- Even where actors share a common collective interest, 'free-riding' is likely to militate against collective action in the absence of other incentives
- Where such collective-action dilemmas can be overcome, powerful interest groups will deploy 'rent-seeking' behaviour, lobbying for monopoly powers and subsidies that are inefficient

Key concepts
- Rationality
- Collective-action problems
- 'Free-riding'
- 'Rent-seeking'

Limitations
- Limited attention given to preference formation
- Limited attention given to the institutional contexts in which rationality is exercised
- Relies upon a series of implausible theoretical assumptions
- Deals poorly with contexts in which altruism and collectively rational behaviour is displayed

Key advocates and seminal works
- Anthony Downs, *Economic Theory of Democracy* (1957)
- Mancur Olson, *The Logic of Collective Action* (1965)
- James Buchanan and Gordon Tullock, *The Calculus of Consent* (1962)

Source: Abridged from Hay 2002: 9.

social world, believing that society was made up of parts – each with its own function – which, like the human body, were interlinked with and interdependent on other parts to form a whole. Such a biological analogy was often used in the writings of functionalism's leading advocates (see Calhoun et al. 2002a: 359–65).

We need to remain aware that 'functionalism', like so many concepts in the human sciences, is notoriously slippery. It refers both to a broader perspective and a substantive or grand theory (see chapter 6 for more on this), and although you may not find many functionalists today, it is useful to understand the roots of this influential perspective.

Table 5 INTERNATIONAL RELATIONS: REALISM

Key assumptions
- Politics is governed by 'objective laws that have their roots in human nature' (Morgenthau 1973: 4)
- The pursuit of power by individual and states is ubiquitous and unavoidable, and conflict and competion are endemic
- In international relations the state is sovereign and the natural unit of analysis

Key themes
- The study of international relations is the study of the interaction between sovereign states
- The self-interested behaviour of states in the absence of any overarching authority on a global scale produces a condition of anarchy

Key concepts
- National interest
- Balance of power
- Sovereignty
- Security

Limitations
- Limited attention to the role of state actors
- Narrowly state-centric
- Relies on an impoverished conception of human nature and implausible assumptions

Key advocates and seminal works
- E. H. Carr, *The Twenty Years' Crisis* (1939)
- Hans Morgenthau, *Politics Among Nations* (1948)

Source: Abridged from Hay 2002: 18–19.

The final perspective under the 'positivist' umbrella is historical empiricism. This is also a disciplinary perspective which, in part, draws heavily on the core tenets of positivism (it must be said that the majority of historical empiricists are not positivists, but for this example we will look at those who are. Empiricism itself is generally understood as an even broader category than positivism; see Robson 2002: 20).

Empiricism, as a philosophical theory, attributes the origin of all knowledge to experience through our senses. As we have seen, this fits with positivism's emphasis on verificational and observable 'facts'. Although historians are what could be termed 'methodologically loose', with many denying that they belong to any perspective whatsoever (Fulbrook 2002: 4), historical empiricism has long been seen as a major perspective within the discipline.

Table 6 SOCIOLOGY: FUNCTIONALISM (SOMETIMES REFERRED TO AS STRUCTURAL-FUNCTIONALISM)

Key assumptions
- Believes that society consists of several parts that work together to achieve stability and solidarity
- Sociology ought to be concerned with analysing these parts and their relationship to each other and society more widely
- Emphasises the importance of *moral consensus* in maintaining order and stability in society

Key themes
- To analyse the manner in which society relates to its many parts, the roles these parts play and how they relate to one another
- A central focus is the study of institutions and their function in society (see Giddens 2001: 16–17)

Key concepts
- Social cohesion
- Stability
- Order

Limitations
- Does not allow for divisions or inequality in society
- Attributes to societies social qualities they do not have
- Other societal factors, like race, class, etc., are neglected

Key figures and seminal works
- Auguste Comte, *A General View of Positivism* (1863)
- Émile Durkheim, *Suicide. A Study in Sociology* (1897)
- Talcott Parsons, *The Social System* (1951)
- Robert Merton, *Social Theory and Social Structure* (1957)

▶ Summary: Disciplines, perspectives, discourses and interdisciplinarity

The discussion in the last section has, I hope, drawn attention to the fact that within disciplinary boundaries we find perspectives that share many common philosophical roots. We could extend the examples above and the results would be the same; for example, in geography you have 'positivist geographers', whose work drew directly from positivism. Pioneering geographers developed quantitative research strategies and searched for scientific laws to explain society from empirically observed particulars (see Hoggart et al. 2002: 5; Johnston et al. 2000: 606–8). The difference between these disciplines is the focus of their study, not necessarily the manner in which they study them.

Table 7 History: Empiricism

Key assumptions
- Believes that there is a 'truth' that is recoverable, that the 'facts speak for themselves'
- Seeks to discern laws of social development from observations about a real external world
- Generally teleological, and often linked to metanarratives

Key themes
- To reconstruct the past based on its traces, on evidence that is real (Fulbrook 2002: 24–5)

Key concepts
- Descriptive narrative
- Gradual change
- Inductive reasoning
- Nominalism

Limitations
- Dichotomy of structure vs. agency
- Often excludes minorities, in particular the 'poor', because of availability of sources and records
- Tends to ignore concepts such as patriarchal structures and cultural influences
- An emphasis on particular instances often loses sight of the 'bigger picture'

Key figures and seminal works
- G. M. Trevelyan, *England Under Queen Anne* (3 vols, 1930–40)
- G. R. Elton, *The Tudor Revolution in Government* (1953)

Despite this, at times it would seem that different disciplines speak a different language or discourse when describing the same event. It is important to know the constraints of particular disciplines, so as to understand that other types of explanation, whether they are theoretical or ontological in form, exist outside one's own field. I fully endorse Andrew Sayer's cutting comments on disciplines when he suggests that 'Disciplinary parochialism, and its close relative disciplinary imperialism, are a recipe for reductionism, blinkered interpretations, and misattributions of causality' (2000: 7).

Academic disciplines do differ in the emphasis they place on the role and position of theory in research, with political science, especially American political science, stressing the need for theory and hypotheses in the pre-empirical stage; that is, *before* research begins. This is standard practice in American graduate schools and is seen as good, solid 'science'. An overemphasis on theory-building can, however, lead the researcher to lose sight of what it is she is meant to be studying.

Moving beyond one's own discipline, and its discourse, is to transcend the familiar; you can liken it to crossing national borders. For example, take my father, who is happy to stay in Britain where he is familiar with the frames of reference, terms, terminology, signs, culture, social habits, language, beer – especially beer – food, traditions and his socio-economic place in society. It is much easier for him to remain in his familiar environment than to have to move to somewhere unfamiliar and learn all of the above from scratch. For this reason he stays where he is and happily criticises the rest. This may be transferred to the academic world by considering someone who remains strictly within disciplinary boundaries, a person who is not receptive to input from other disciplines. In this case, our academic would criticise from a position of ignorance and deny herself the chance of exposure to different frames of reference, terms and terminology, and different traditions and world-views. She would be at a loss, for it is these experiences that we take back to, and which enrich, our own disciplinary training (incidentally, this unwillingness to 'travel' can also be the case *within* a discipline, for example political science, where competing approaches to the study of politics coexist). This is not to suggest that you ought to be proactively 'interdisciplinary', but rather that, by looking beyond disciplinary boundaries, you as researchers are often forced to reassess your 'taken-for-granted' assumptions – good practice in scholarship and a guard against disciplinary entrenchment.

▶ Interdisciplinarity' or 'post-disciplinarity'

The debate on interdisciplinarity is often very confusing, especially as the term itself is misused and lumped together with transdisciplinarity, cross-disciplinarity and multidisciplinarity. One way of thinking of the debate is to imagine a continuum which runs from multidisciplinarity on the one hand, where different scholars focus on the same area of study but remain strictly within their various disciplinary boundaries, to the utopian ideal of post-disciplinarity on the other, in which no disciplinary boundaries are recognised, or transdisciplinarity, in which we all learn each others' trade. To paraphrase one well-known thinker, the latter is a scenario where in the morning we do complex regression analysis, in the afternoon undertake some discourse analysis of literary texts and finish off the day assessing the use of the ideal type 'totalitarianism' for capturing the key features of the Nazi dictatorship! The utopian ideal of transdisciplinarity, and the loose manner in which the concept of interdisciplinarity is employed, is to be avoided, given the fact that it is hard enough for students to master the tools of *one* discipline fully in the short space of time afforded to studying at tertiary level (see Dogan 2000: 98). It is better to speak of 'cross-fertilisation' between disciplines, whereby scholars learn from one another, share methods of research, and are willing to accept different interpretations of events. Equally, as Dogan rightly points out, using the example of his discipline: 'The relations between political science and the other social sciences are in reality *relations between sectors of different disciplines, not between whole disciplines.* It is not an 'interdisciplinary' endeavour ... . The current advancement of the social sciences can be explained in large part by the hybridization of segments of sciences (ibid.: 97, my emphasis). The point of this final section is to suggest that a willingness to look across disciplinary boundaries, and to develop and readjust our own points of view, is beneficial to scholarship as a whole. For it is at these junctures – that is, at the areas of overlap between the disciplines – that interdisciplinary exchange, or a dialectic between disciplines, takes place. The aim is not the knitting together of disciplines in a seamless mass of interpretation and explanation, but rather the sharing of insights, best practice and methods with other disciplines. There is less a need for specific training in a range of different disciplines, than an open mind when approaching research. Interestingly enough, we can extend this idea of cross-fertilisation and overlap to the discussion of perspectives above, as some of the most fruitful research undertaken is that which is, for example, neither neatly within a 'critical realist' nor an 'interpretivist' tradition, but that which lies along the fault line between both.

▶ Summary

The key points to take away from this chapter are:

- All research takes place within a research paradigm, whether it is explicitly stated or not.
- The key research paradigms in the human sciences are positivism, (critical) realism and interpretivism.
- Remember that these paradigms are not clear-cut and much of the best research takes place on the borders between them (note: positivism and interpretivism cannot be used together).

- Different disciplinary perspectives draw from similar ontological and epistemological roots and share similar foundational assumptions, thereby rendering blurry the often sharp distinction between disciplines made in academia.
- In order to assist the reading around your topic, familiarise yourself with the range of disciplinary perspectives in table 7 and with post-modernism and feminism.
- Be prepared to look beyond your own perspective and your own discipline and see how other researchers undertake their work.

▶ Essential reading

Guba, E. G. and Lincoln, Y. S. (1998) 'Competing Paradigms in Qualitative Research', in N. K. Denzin and Y. S. Lincoln (eds), *The Landscape of Qualitative Research*, Thousand Oaks, CA, London and New Delhi, Sage.

Hollis, M. (1994) *The Philosophy of Social Science, an Introduction*, Cambridge, Cambridge University Press, chapter 3.

Hughes, J. and Sharrock, W. (1997) *The Philosophy of Social Research*, London, New York, Longman, 3rd edn, various chapters.

Marsh, D. and Stoker, G. (eds) (2002) *Theory and Methods in Political Science*, Basingstoke, Palgrave Macmillan, updated and revised edn, chapter 1.

Sayer, A. (2000) *Realism and Social Science*, London, Sage, part I.

▶ Further reading

Bryman, A. (2001) *Social Research Methods*, Oxford, Oxford University Press, chapter 1.

Delanty, G. (2000) *Social Science. Beyond Constructivism and Realism*, Buckingham, Open University Press, various chapters.

Hay, C. (2002) *Political Analysis*, Basingstoke, Palgrave Macmillan, chapter 1.

Jenkins, R. (2002) *Foundations of Sociology*, Basingstoke, Palgrave Macmillan, chapter 1.

6 The Types and Uses of Theory in Research

This chapter introduces you to 'theory' and its uses in research by:

- Offering an introductory discussion of theory and your project
- Giving an overview of the 'dominant' understanding of theory in research
- Problematising this view by showing how different research traditions use and understand theory
- Discussing the uses of theory in research, ranging from 'metatheory' through 'middle-range theory' to 'grounded theory'
- Presenting the so-called 'inductive – deductive' dichotomy in building theory and undertaking research

This chapter focuses on the concept of '**theory**' in social research. My intention is to provide you with a discussion of the meaning and purpose of theory in social research and the variety of uses of theory you are likely to encounter. Understanding the meaning and purpose of theory is very important for undergraduates, necessary for postgraduates and crucial for those undertaking doctoral studies. As I have suggested, the human sciences today are characterised by a confused, misused and inconsistent lexicon of key terms and components of research, made worse by the lack of agreement and use across academic disciplines. The official name of this widespread problem is, according to Gerring (2001: 65), 'homonymy (multiple meanings for the same term)' and 'synonymy (different terms with the same, or overlapping, meanings)'.

While many core concepts in the human sciences have a generic meaning that can travel across disciplines, 'theory' is less easy to pin down. This is due to the role theory plays in social research, a role complicated by the fact that it is utilised for different purposes by different academic perspectives working in different philosophical traditions within the human sciences. As we shall see, the meaning and role of theory in social research changes according to individual scholars' ontological and epistemological positions. These positions operate with – at times – incompatible conceptions of what theory is and what role in research it may perform.

There are several other reasons for the confusion surrounding the term 'theory'. First, the variety of uses of theory in different contexts makes it impossible to fix its meaning. Secondly, the propensity of some academics and students to collapse the concept of theory together with the other classificatory tools such as 'ideal type', 'model', 'typology' and even 'concept' discussed in chapter 2 has added to a lack of understanding of the term. Thirdly, its use in popular parlance, as in 'Well, in theory that's OK, but in practice . . .', has added to the confusion, as Robert Merton's classic statement succinctly sums up: 'Like so many words that are bandied about, the word theory threatens to become meaningless. Because its referents are so diverse – including everything from minor working hypotheses, through comprehensive but vague and unordered speculations, to axiomatic systems of thought – use of the word often obscures rather than creates understanding' (Merton 1967: 39). Finally, the dominant understanding of theory and its application in research has been strongly influenced by the positivist research tradition and deductivism (Bryman 2001: 8). Positivism itself has been heavily influenced by the role of theory in natural science, the so-called 'scientific method' discussed briefly in chapter 5. In the natural sciences, theories are seen as possible explanations which can be tested and they often contain replicable relationships between certain variables (that is, concepts which vary in amount or kind – even this type of language would not be accepted by other research traditions, as we have seen). Rarely in the human sciences, however, do we encounter such replicable and reliable 'laws' – in fact I cannot think of any – although, as we shall see below, some scholars working within the positivist research tradition may attempt to approximate science and its laws.

The chapter proceeds by way of a general introduction to the topic of 'theory' and its relevance to your project. I then offer an overview of the traditional and dominant definition of theory in social research which rests firmly on the 'scientific method'. The following section problematises this traditional understanding of theory by discussing the role assigned to it – and offering examples of the use of theory – by the key social research traditions (positivism, post-positivism (critical realism), interpretivism and post-modernism). The final section discusses the most common uses of theory in research, which ranges from metatheory, through middle-range theory to grounded theory. Each of these will be illuminated by way of an example of how they are employed in research.

▶ Introducing theory

The first thing to remember is that you should not use theory for the sake of it. One common mistake in students' projects is a lack of connection between the theoretical section, the purpose of which is to shed light on the empirical reality, and the actual research undertaken, with the result that both sections could, in fact, stand on their own. The purpose of the theoretical part of a dissertation, doctorate or project – and the purpose of good theory – is precisely to give a sense of order to the empirical section, so that the two parts need to be inextricably linked; otherwise, you defeat the object of abstraction, which is to simplify and not complicate further the understanding of complex social phenomena. This does not, of course, apply to purely theoretical projects, which would have to be divided up somewhat differently. Whether to use a specific theory or not will depend on your discipline and your object of study. As always, there is a balance to be found between telling a story of an isolated case with no deeper understanding of the underlying processes of cause and effect, and overburdening the reader by stifling the content with elaborate theoretical considerations. The choice of whether to theorise or not to theorise is not as straightforward as it may at first seem, because *all* research is necessarily embedded in some form of theoretical framework. However, there is pressure on you to use a specific 'theory' because it looks good, sounds sophisticated and indicates that you can get your head around the hard stuff. However, a 'bolted-on' theoretical section, which is not integrated or interlinked with the empirical section, is likely to end in a failed dissertation or a referred thesis at the viva stage or, worse still, complete failure!

There is no general consensus on the role of theory in research precisely because of the different ontological starting points of researchers. However, most academics attempting to *explain* complex social phenomena – as opposed to *describing* them in detail – agree that some form of framework is necessary to assist in both selecting and prioritising certain factors over others and in showing relationships between certain concepts at an abstract level. Thus, so the argument goes, by abstract connection of theoretical concepts *with observation*, the concepts gain in empirical meaning. This is why many researchers insist that empirical evidence ought to be tangible, measurable or observable, as much theory in the human sciences attempts to link observables with other observables, except, as we have seen, those based on either a 'realist' or 'anti-foundationalist' ontology, which seek to uncover structures and mechanisms that cannot always be seen. This simplification of reality is deemed by many as necessary if we are to achieve any kind of overview and weighting of certain variables and their effect on others. Gerry Stoker neatly sums up this viewpoint by suggesting that theory

> helps us to see the wood for the trees. Good theories select out certain factors as the most important or relevant if one is interested in providing an explanation of an event. Without such a sifting process no effective observation can take place. The observer would be buried under a pile of detail and be unable to weigh the influence of different factors in explaining an event. Theories are of value precisely because they structure all observations. (Stoker 1995: 16–17)

Structuring our observations in a long piece of work is seen as vital if we are under time constraints. Students rarely have the luxury of simply gathering information and data in the hope of discovering specific patterns and relationships between phenomena. It is more likely that their ideas will already be informed by previous research and theories, discussions with peers and supervisors, and 'gut' feelings which all help, at an early stage, to identify general research questions (see below for a discussion of 'inductive' and 'deductive' research).

Put simply, 'Theories are nets cast to catch what we call "the world": to rationalise, to explain and to master it. We endeavour to make the mesh ever finer and finer' (Popper 2000: 59). Without theory, or at least some form of classificatory system, it would be extremely difficult to know which data and facts to collect in the first place. Even researchers setting out to generate theory from fieldwork have to start with some assumptions based on a certain level of abstraction. Another thing to note about theory at this early stage is that it comes in many diverse forms, ranging from grand theory and middle-range theory to grounded theory (see below for a thorough examination of types of theory and its uses in research).

Remember, too, that theories are, of course, bound up with certain ways of seeing the world, so you need to remain vigilant and on the lookout for interesting social phenomena which your theories may actually steer you away from.

Let us now turn to the common or dominant understanding of just what theory is and what it is good for.

▶ The traditional view of theory

Reach once again for your trusty dictionary – the one that failed to help us clarify 'ontology' and 'epistemology' – and you will find a definition of theory similar to the following: theory is 'a scheme or system of ideas or statements held as an *explanation* or *account* of a group of facts or phenomena... a statement of what are held to be general laws, principles, or causes of something known or observed (*Shorter Oxford English Dictionary*, cited in Blaikie 2000: 141, my emphasis). This definition is clearly based on a traditional view of the natural sciences. It suggests that a theory is an explanation *or* account of a group of facts. As we shall see, different research traditions will understand theory as either explanatory or descriptive but rarely both.

In general, theories are understood as abstract notions which assert specific relationships between concepts. The abstract ideas and propositions contained in theory are either tested in fieldwork by the collection of data or derive from the data itself. Following Popper (1959, 2000: 40–3), theory ought to be 'falsifiable'; that is, it 'must be possible *in principle* to falsify a theory' (Gilbert 2001: 20). If it is not possible to falsify, then it is by definition not a theory (ibid.: 20). (As we shall see below, the concept of falsifiability is not without problems, if we understand 'theory' in a broader sense than that sketched here.) A good theory will be generalisable – and, if possible, predictive – and able to be employed in different contexts to the original.

In the strictest sense, a theory consists of a 'system of statements that encompass a number of hypotheses or laws' (Schnell et al. 1999: 52). Laws in this case relate more to natural-science subjects, where tests are replicated again and again to produce the same results. There are very few instances of such laws in the 'messy' social sciences and humanities, as the study of people, their institutions, their environment and their creative output is a very complex task, and one which is made more difficult by the multitude of factors that go into making up social phenomena. Instead, sets of hypotheses link together to create a theory.

In actual research, scholars usually test these hypotheses rather than the complete theory itself (Silverman 2000: 78), although, as Hay (2002: 84) shrewdly notes, it is 'impossible to test single hypotheses in isolation from others', as all are related to further presumptions. Hypotheses are traditionally linked to the *deductive* method of research (Blaikie 2000: 163), yet this distinction is only of limited use, as we shall discuss below.

As we saw in chapter 3, a hypothesis itself is a proposition, set of propositions or an assumption put forward for empirical testing; a testable proposition about the relationship between two or more events or concepts. Hypotheses consist of (at the very least) an independent and dependent variable and usually contain a causal proposition. They are made up of concepts – the building blocks of theories – which have been turned into variables (this process is usually termed 'operationalising').

The remainder of this chapter will problematise the above conception of theory in social research by turning to perhaps the most important question of all: the role of theory in social research.

▶ The role of theory in social research

The above understanding of theory fails to take into account three key factors. First, all research is necessarily based on some assumptions about the nature of social reality and what we can know about it. As Ben Rosamond correctly states, 'we are all' – whether we like it or not – 'informed by theoretical perspectives, even if we adopt an avowedly non-theoretical posture' (2000: 4–5). This is what we discussed in chapter 4 – the starting point of all research. Thus, 'theory' permeates all research. Secondly, the fact that different research traditions have different understandings of theory means that the narrow positivist definition presented above is simply one of many legitimate definitions of theory (see below for an outline of how positivists view the *role* of theory in research). Thirdly, the variety of uses of theory in social research adds another dimension to the problem of its definition, for it can be grand theory or grounded theory, metatheory or middle-range theory. It is to these factors that we now turn.

▶ Research paradigms and the role of theory

If you are to reflect convincingly upon the theory which inevitably informs your work, you need a clearer understanding of its meaning and its purpose in the study of social phenomena. The terms in this section are used to denote very broad research traditions within which a wide variety of perspectives exist – outlined in chapter 5 – that are qualitatively different from one another. The aim now is to introduce you to, and offer an outline of, the role of theory within these positions.

The positivist paradigm

The rationalist side of positivism applies a deductive research strategy and sees theory as a tool to 'order, explain and predict facts' (Danermark et al. 2002: 116). A theory is seen by researchers working in this paradigm as useful only if it can generate testable (and preferably falsifiable) hypotheses (Hay 2002: 37). The most hard-nosed among rationalists would understand the role of theory as being predictive and consisting of interconnected causal laws. Thus, theory for rationalists serves to 'simplify an external reality as a condition of the generation of predictive hypotheses' (Hay 2002: 39).

Box 29   Positivist theory: rational choice

A key example of such a theory in this tradition is Rational Choice Theory (RCT), used most frequently in sociology, political science, economics and international relations. RCT, for example, 'assumes that all political actors maximize their own personal utility, or self interest, when choosing between alternatives' (Landman 2000: 15). RCT should be looked upon as an approach to social phenomena and not as a specific theory as such. Nonetheless, the core assumptions that underlie the mainstream version of RCT (as described in chapter 5) are similar and will be similar across the wide variety of applications of this type of analysis.

Behaviouralism, on the other hand, while sharing many of the assumptions found under the broad church of positivism, employs an inductive research strategy, by deriving theories and generalisations from empirical evidence. Theory for this group is a way of recording the patterns directly observed in empirical data. Theory is not used to direct initial research by generating hypotheses to be tested in the field; rather, theory is built out of the observational data recorded by these researchers (see Hay 2002: 41–5 for a thorough overview of behaviouralism).

The (critical) realist paradigm

Realism as an ontological position covers a very wide range of perspectives from a number of academic disciplines. However, in general it can be said that realists tend to use theory to guide their research and to interpret the facts they find. Like positivists – but unlike interpretivists – most realists believe in the possibility of causal explanation (Sayer 2000: 6; Marsh and Furlong 2002: 30; Delanty 2000: 129). The purpose of theory in this tradition – and in particular for the more recent variety of approach termed 'critical realism' – is to uncover the deep underlying structures of social reality by 'identifying generative mechanisms' (Delanty 2000: 130–1) that cannot necessarily be seen but can be identified (Hollis and Smith 1990: 207). For critical realists, reality does not present itself as it really is; thus in order to 'reveal the structured reality of the world we inhabit, we must cast our gaze beyond the superficial world of appearances, deploying theory as a sensitising device to reveal the structured reality beneath the surface. It is this "depth ontology" which underpins critical realism' (Hay 2002: 122).

Box 30   Theory for realists

for the realist, a scientific theory is a description of structures and mechanisms which causally generate the observable phenomena, a description which enables us to explain them. (Keat and Urry 1978: 5, cited in Danermark et al. 2002: 120)

The term patriarchy offers an instructive example of a realist approach to social phenomena. Partriachy, according to its Marxist variant, 'argues that material structures determine relations between men and women' (Cannell and Green 2001: 592). These structures are produced by capitalism and 'function to serve the interests of capital' (Abercrombie et al. 1984: 155), and, while it is difficult to observe directly the underlying causes of patriarchy, it is possible to point to its consequences in society. Take, for example, the percentage of professors at your university who are female: it is *very* likely that the percentage of male professors is well over double that of the females. There could be a number of explanations for this, but it is quite clear that the committees charged with promotion to professorships are made up overwhelmingly of male, middle-class *men*. The composition of such committees could be understood as an end result of a process of structural patriarchy that might not otherwise be visible.

The interpretivist paradigm

Researchers working in this tradition tend to see theory as deriving from data collection and not as the driving force of research. According to interpretivists, theory helps us understand the social world (they tend not to believe that theory can be predictive) by describing and interpreting how people conduct their daily lives (Neuman 2000: 73). Thus, as the study of social phenomena is different from that of the natural sciences, using deductive theory (i.e. theories that inform research at the outset and hypotheses which stipulate the type of evidence we ought to look for) is not adequate to capture the complexities of social phenomena. Many interpretivists would not subscribe to the notion of 'testing' a theory in the field, but would rather be looking to 'build' theory from the data (see, in particular, 'grounded theory' below).

Box 31 Theory in the interpretivist tradition

A good example of a theory in this tradition is Max Weber's *Protestant Ethic and the Spirit of Capitalism*, in which he highlights the link between religious ideas and economic institutions. Calhoun et al. 2002b: 168 summarise this as follows:

Weber argues that a particular form of ascetic Protestantism fostered a 'spirit' of modern capitalism, marked by a ceaseless obligation to earn money and to reinvest for profit .... The emergence of Protestantism in Europe was partially related to economic factors, Weber argued, but this could not explain the relationship between ascetic Protestantism and capitalism in the 'backwoods' of early America .... In this case, a religious idea motivating the actions of individuals had a major world-historical effect on the economic structure.

The post-modernist paradigm

It is questionable whether post-modernism is a research paradigm or not. It is certainly an ontological position which views the 'core' ontological and epistemological positions in the human sciences with some scepticism. Nonetheless, its recent ascent in the fields of cultural studies, sociology, political science and international relations means we need to pay attention to what those researchers, who identify themselves as post-modernist, say. Post-modernism could be summed up as a purely theoretical narrative in its own right. Post-modernists would probably not wish to use the same language as the 'mainstream' epistemological positions introduced above in the first place; instead they would 'deconstruct' the assumptions and terminology they employ. Researchers working in this tradition certainly do not believe in a 'predictive' role for theory in research (Crotty 1998), although they do suggest that theories (especially influential ones) can become self-fulfilling prophecies. Finally, post-modernists do not believe that 'grand theories' (for example, Marxism and functionalism; see below) have any relevance today (Jones 2002: 224; see Chapter 5 for an explanation of 'post-modernism').

▶ Different uses of theory

You need to be aware of the variety of theories used in social research, ranging from metatheory, grand and middle-range theory to grounded theory. The difference between these theories is their degree of abstraction, their scope and the level of social reality they deal with. Figure 3 below sets out these theories on a continuum running from 'abstract' on one end to 'empirical' on the other. This is an artificial breakdown of macro- and micro-theory intended only as an overview of the key uses of theory in the human sciences.

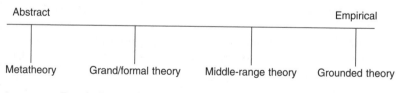

FIGURE 3 DIFFERENT USES OF THEORY IN SOCIAL RESEARCH

Metatheory
This term pertains to the foundational assumptions and philosophical underpinnings of *all* research. As I have outlined above, the key

epistemological positions in social science – themselves based on specific ontological assumptions – would be included under this broad heading (see also Danermark et al. 2002: 118). Examples in this category are an interpretivist epistemology founded on an anti-foundationalist ontology and a positivist epistemology based on a foundationalist ontology. Ontological assumptions – upon which all theories are based – are not in and of themselves verifiable or falsifiable (Grix 2002b; Hay 2002). Some scholars have argued that 'metatheory' 'should be settled before theorizing begins' (Blaikie 2000: 154). This is true in as much as scholars and students need to be explicit about their ontological and epistemological assumptions, as it is these which inform the rest of the research design, including the level, reach and importance of theory.

Grand or formal theories

Grand theories are generally rather speculative and abstract (Danermark et al. 2002: 125) and are 'intended to represent the important features of a total society' (Blaikie 2000: 144).

Box 32   Grand theory – functionalism

A good example of a grand theory is that of 'functionalism'. Functionalism, one of the key perspectives in sociology (see chapter 5 for an overview), suggests that society consists of several parts that work together to achieve stability and solidarity (Giddens 2001: 16). It is the job of sociology to study these individual parts, and their relationship to one another and to society as a whole. Talcott Parsons's attempt at a 'theory of social systems' fits into this category (Parsons 1948: 156–63, reprinted in Calhoun et al. 2002b: 359–65). Parsons went on to describe society as being made up of three interdependent systems: a 'cultural', a 'personality' and a 'social' system (ibid.: 343). It is not difficult to see how employing such a theory in actual research might be difficult, given its vast scope.

In contrast to the more practical 'middle-range' theories, the theory informing such a perspective attempts to encapsulate a whole society. Such theories tend to be transhistorical; that is, they are not strictly limited to time and space.

Middle-range theories (or 'substantive theories')

Middle-range theories, probably the most commonly used in social science research – and probably the most likely to be used by students – are limited to, and developed for, a specific area of social concern (Neuman 2000: 51); for example, the labour process (Bryman 2001: 6) or race relations. Robert Merton, who coined this term, believed that middle-range theory built on the work of classical theoretical formulations (Blaikie 2000: 148).

Middle-range theories should be specific enough to be used to guide empirical work, but broad enough to cover a wide range of different phenomena (Giddens 2001: 664).

Box 33   Middle-range theory

Durkheim's theory of suicide (originally published in 1897) is probably one of the most widely cited examples of a theory of the middle range. Basically, Durkheim sets out to show how the social world impacts on the personal and individual experience of suicide. He discovered certain 'patterns' among specific socio-economic groups (male, female, wealthy, poor, etc.), noting the differences in suicide rates. He also discovered that the rate of suicide varied, with lower figures during wartime and higher rates during times of economic change. The result of these findings was the conclusion that social forces external to the individual affected rates of suicide (based on the summary in Giddens 2001: 10–11).

Grounded theory

This term, coined by B. G. Glaser and A. L. Strauss in the 1960s, is generally associated with inductive research strategies. **Grounded theory** can be understood as an attempt to close the gap between theory and research (by 'grounding' theory in empirical data). Researchers seek relationships between concepts among the data they have collected and 'code' the data shortly after initial data collection and interpretation. The idea is to approach the data *without* any preconceived categories or codes. Grounded theory does not start out with hypotheses, but develops them after collecting initial data. This type of research involves the interpretation of data in their social and cultural context and sets out to

112 The Foundations of Research

'construct abstract theory about that data, which is grounded in the data. The concepts which the theory will use are not brought to the data and are not likely to be obvious in the data' (Punch 2000a: 218).

Box 34 The aim of grounded theory

According to Holloway's useful book of concepts, the main aim of grounded theory is:

the generation of theory from the data, although existing theories can be modified or extended through this approach. It emphasises the development of ideas from the data like other qualitative methods but goes further than these. Grounded theory researchers start with an area of interest, collect the data and allow the relevant ideas to develop.

Rigid preconceived ideas prevent development of the research; imposing a framework might block the awareness of major concepts that emerge from the data. Grounded theory is especially useful in situations where little is known about a particular topic or problem area, or where a new and exciting outlook is needed in familiar settings. (Holloway 1997: 80–7)

Grounded theory is known more for its *process*, i.e. how it develops theory via carefully planned steps (Crotty 1998: 78), than for actual applicable theories themselves (see Bryman 2001: 387–404 for a full exposition) and can be looked upon as a *'general methodology* for developing theory that is grounded in data systematically gathered and analyzed' (Strauss and Corbin 1998: 158).

Box 35 Summary of what theory is and the role it plays in research

Now, it is obviously difficult to give a succint summary of just what theory is and the role it plays in research given the numerous viewpoints and uses of theory highlighted above, not all of which are compatible with one another. However, I can offer some general points relating to theory and its purpose in your projects:

* To give structure and direction to your endeavours by pointing you to specific 'variables' (be aware of the things that you are being pointed away from).

- Theory is a specific language with which to describe and explain the social world we study.
- Theory is an abstraction of reality, in which concepts – with referents in the 'real' world – are related to other concepts, offering us tentative hypotheses or explanations.
- Different uses of theory exist and operate at different 'levels', for example, 'grand theory' and 'middle-range theory'.
- *All* research is underpinned by 'metatheoretical' assumptions; even if we do not believe in theory at all, we are still taking a 'theoretical' stance on research.
- A multitude of specific theories operate within these metatheoretical frameworks.

▶ Inductive and deductive theory and research

The final section of this chapter turns your attention to the perennial problem of induction vs. deduction. Very simply, induction refers to 'the process by which conclusions are drawn from direct observation of empirical evidence' (Landman 2000: 226). These conclusions are then fed into the development of theory. Such research is not hypotheses-driven; instead, theory is generated and built through the analysis of, and interaction with, the empirical data. The researcher looks for patterns in the data and, in particular, relationships between variables. Generalisations in this type of research are sought from the *specific* to other, wider contexts, as opposed to deductive research strategies (see below). This type of research and theory is usually, but not exclusively, associated with the interpretivist research tradition and qualitative research strategies.

Deductive theory and research, on the other hand, is a type of strategy in which theory informs research at the outset and hypotheses dictate what evidence the researcher looks for. Data are then collected to confirm or falsify the hypotheses. Deductive theories, in contrast to inductive theories, 'arrive at their conclusions by applying reason to a given set of premises.... For example, the rational-choice perspective in political science assumes that all political actors maximize their own personal utility, or self-interest, when choosing between alternatives' (Landman 2000: 15). A further classic example of a **deductive research** strategy is that advocated by the American political scientists, King, Keohane and Verba (1994: 29; emphasis added):

Any theory that does real work for us has implications for empirical investigations; *no empirical investigation can be successful without theory to guide its choice of questions*... social science conclusions cannot be considered reliable if they are not based on theory and data in strong connection with one another and forged by formulating and examining the observable implication of a theory.

King et al. seem to imply that there is no room for an **inductive research** strategy. However, like other doubtful dichotomies in the human sciences – for example, that between quantitative and qualitative research methods and research strategies discussed in chapter 7 – the distinction between inductive and deductive research and theory is useful only up to a point. It is good to distinguish between the underlying logic of research, yet the distinction between inductive and deductive theory is made more complicated if we consider the following. If I take a newly-formed grounded theory as the starting point for my research project, am I now using a theory formed inductively or deductively? Or is it, as I suspect, simply not possible (nor desirable?) to have no *a priori* assumptions before I begin my research? Is not all research to some extent deductive? Here I agree with Ragin (1994: 47), who suggests that, in reality, most research uses both induction and deduction, as there is a necessary *interplay* between ideas and evidence in each research process (see also Gilbert 2001: 20 and May 2001: 34–5).

Box 36 To deduct or to induct?

While the deduction – induction distinction is a simple and appealing way to differentiate kinds of social research, most research includes elements of both. For this reason some philosophers of science argue that all research involves retroduction – the interplay of induction and deduction. It is impossible to do research without some initial ideas ... almost all research has at least an element of deduction .... Research involves deduction because there is typically a dialogue of ideas and evidence in social research. The interaction of ideas and evidence culminates in theoretically based descriptions of social life. (Ragin 1994: 47)

It is this reflexivity – moving constantly between concrete data and abstraction and back again – that you ought to strive to achieve in your studies.

▶ **Summary**

This chapter has offered a discussion of the meaning and purpose of theory in social research. To summarise:

- I argued that you do not need a *specific* theory to undertake research, although *all* research is underpinned by metatheoretical assumptions.
- I introduced the traditional understanding of 'theory', which has been influenced by the positivist research tradition, which in turn has been heavily influenced by the 'scientific method'.
- I then problematised the notion of 'one' understanding of theory and its role in research by introducing different research traditions and their use of theory.
- I briefly discussed the variety of theories in research, all of which have different purposes.
- Finally, I introduced you to yet another dichotomy in research, that between 'inductive' and 'deductive' research, suggesting that while the term may be useful to distinguish between certain research strategies, the vast majority of research combines both induction and deduction.

▶ **Essential reading**

Blaikie, N. (2000) *Designing Social Research*, Cambridge, Polity Press.
Gilbert, N. (ed.) (2001) *Researching Social Life*, London, Sage, chapter 2.
Jones, D. (2002) 'Contemporary Theorising', in I. Marsh (ed.), *Theory and Practice in Sociology*, Harlow, Prentice Hall, pp. 220–56.

▶ **Further reading**

Bryman, A. (2001) *Social Research Methods*, Oxford, Oxford University Press.
Neuman, W. L. (2000) *Social Research Methods. Qualitative and Quantitative Approaches*, Boston, MA, Allyn & Bacon, 4th edn.

7 Introducing Research Methods

Chapter 7 introduces:

- The nature of quantitative and qualitative research strategies
- Criticisms of both types of strategy
- The so-called quantitative–qualitative dichotomy
- A range of the most common research methods used in research projects
- A brief discussion on mixing methods and data ('triangulation')

The language associated with research methods in the human sciences is the topic of this chapter. Instead of simply listing the types of methods that are available for you to use in your projects, the organising principle of this chapter is the so-called 'quantitative–qualitative' research dichotomy. So, this will be a recurring theme throughout, as I first offer a brief overview of both research strategies, adding a short summary of the most common criticisms and limitations of each. Then I turn to the dichotomy itself and pose the question of whether this is a false antithesis or not. As I shall be at pains to point out, I believe that the distinction between quantitative and qualitative research strategies is useful, but the methods associated with each, indeed, the logic of **inference** underlying both types of enquiry, may be the same, rendering the sharp distinction between them that is often made a false one (Landman 2000: 19; Silverman 2000: 11). Equally, both qualitative and quantitative research must be understood as umbrella terms, under which a wide and diverse range of 'paradigms, approaches to data, and methods for the analysis of data' are categorised (Punch 2000b: 139).

Before highlighting the important debate surrounding mixing methods or 'triangulation', something you need to digest before embarking on your dissertation or thesis, I offer an overview of the most frequently used research methods in the human sciences, their potential and their limitations.

▶ Quantitative research

Broadly speaking, quantitative research is characterised by three basic phases: finding **variables** for concepts, operationalising them in the study, and measuring them. This type of research approach tends, in general, to 'abstract from particular instances to seek general description or to test causal hypotheses; it seeks measurements and analyses that are easily replicable by other researchers' (King et al. 1994: 3). (Of course, not all quantification satisfies King's statement, the use of quantitative methods in discourse analysis being a case in point.) The replication of methods is seen by supporters of quantitative analyses as very important, because the work is thus subject to **verifiability**, which provides an air of legitimacy, reproducibility, reliability and objectivity. Statistical reliability is sought by undertaking a random sample of cases (the more the better) from which generalisable results can be gleaned. Therefore, studies employing quantitative methods are more often than not carried out involving a number of cases or subjects, which are independent of context, or, to put it another way, they are studies in which the researcher does not physically interact with the subject of analysis. A case in point would be an analysis based on statistics of several countries' welfare states. These statistics can be collated from various sources, without having to visit the countries involved. In this type of research, the researcher is said to be detached from the object of study (Neuman 2000: 16). Of course, no one can be fully detached from any type of research – or offer a **value-free** analysis – precisely because researchers are the sum of their accumulated knowledge, which is based on certain assumptions about the world.

Quantitative research, pejoratively known as 'number-crunching' (usually by those who can't do it), uses techniques that apply more to numerical data. Researchers develop variables or concepts which can be measured, and convert them into specific data-collection techniques. These techniques produce precise numerical information which can be understood as the empirical representation of the (abstract) concepts (Neuman 2000: 157–8). Quantitative techniques include identifying general patterns and relationships among variables, testing hypotheses and theories, and making predictions based on these results (Ragin

1994: 132–6). Some statistical packages and models require a fairly high level of mathematical knowledge, whilst other packages, for example SPSS (Statistical Package in the Social Sciences), do a lot of the calculations for you. The researcher must, however, be in a position to *interpret* the statistics the program produces. When using statistics, she also needs to be aware of sampling error and the potential biases in any interpretation of findings. The most common types of method associated with quantitative research are social surveys, analyses of previously collected data or official statistics and 'structured' observation (Silverman 2000: 3). Quantitative researchers may seek correlations between variables, but they are often 'reluctant to move from statements of **correlation** to **causal** statements' (ibid.: 4), as the complexity of social life makes it difficult to be absolutely certain if a particular variable is the sole cause of something.

One particular technique, favoured by economists and political scientists, is that of regression analysis and, above all, multiple-regression analysis. The basic idea underlying regression analysis is to 'use some data on one or more variables (for example people's diet and exercise habits) to try to predict the value of a further variable (for example on their general health)' (Wood 2003: 143). Multiple regression, as the name implies, uses a number of variables to make the same prediction or explanation. To understand basic descriptive statistics, the like of which you will find in most quality journals, it is necessary to learn the language of quantitative analysis. Even if you have no intention of using statistics, make sure you read a basic introductory book and familiarise yourself with terms such as 'standard deviation', 'mean', 'median' and 'normal distribution'.

While a firm understanding of the role statistics play in our lives and in much scholarship is essential, whether you intend to employ them in your study or not, you need to be aware that some facets of human action, especially behavioural phenomena, are difficult to capture or 'measure' quantitatively. Many critics of quantitative research are quick to pick up on this, suggesting that 'there are areas of social reality which such statistics cannot measure' (Silverman 2000: 8); an example here would be the concept of trust (see Grix 2001b: 200 and box 37, chapter 2), for which a combination of both quantitative and qualitative research would be more appropriate in order to understand the social and political contexts in which these attitudes and opinions are formed.

Quantitative research strategies use the specific language touched on in chapter 1, in particular the terms 'hypotheses' and 'variables'. Variables include the independent variable ('the cause'), the dependent variable ('the effect') and the control variable (usually 'manipulated' and often called the 'covariate'). Research rests on the observation and measurement of repeated incidences of a social or political phenomenon (a good example is the votes cast for a political party). Such research is usually thought to be grounded in a more 'positivist' philosophical tradition (although, as we have seen, this is not necessarily the case). Quantitative studies are generally interested in comparison and causality (often finding the independent variable(s) which cause variance or change in the dependent variable) and they generally use a *large* number of cases.

Box 37   Criticisms of quantitative research at a glance

Some of the most common and recurring criticisms of quantitative research tend to be the following:

- Researchers using a quantitative research strategy are often reluctant to move from statements of **correlation** to **causal** statements.
- Such a dependence on quantitative methods can lead to a neglect of the social and cultural context in which the 'variable' being 'measured' operates.
- This type of research relies heavily on concepts in the pursuit of 'measurable' phenomena and, as we have seen, it is difficult to match concepts with their referents in the social world (for example, 'trust', 'delinquency', etc.).
- Quantitative research is not value-free, as many of its proponents suggest, as no one can be fully detached from any type of research, precisely because researchers are the sum of their accumulated knowledge, which is based on certain assumptions about the world.
- Critics argue that perhaps there are some facets of human action, especially behavioural phenomena, that are difficult to capture or 'measure' quantitatively.

▶ Qualitative research

Qualitative research is seen by many as almost the complete opposite of quantitative research. It usually involves in-depth investigation of knowledge through, for example, participant observation (as in anthropological fieldwork), employing the interviewing technique, archival or other documentary analyses, or ethnographic study (Ragin 1994: 91). These methods do not rely on, but can involve, numerical measurements.

Different research traditions and the different perspectives within them (like those introduced in chapter 5), have different views about the extent to which empirical research can tell us anything, and, ultimately, different opinions on what we can learn from qualitative research. In general, qualitative researchers tend to be working in an 'interpretivist' philosophical position, using methods of data generation which are flexible and sensitive to the social context in which the data are produced (as opposed to the more 'deskbound' calculations of some quantitative analysis). However, methods associated with qualitative research, interviews, observation, etc., are used frequently by researchers working within a positivist or realist research paradigm. Ethical considerations are thought to be greater for those conducting qualitative research, given the direct contact researchers have with people, their personal lives and the issues of confidentiality that arise out of this.

Furthermore, qualitative researchers generally seek to amass information from their studies on, for example, a particular event, decision, institution, geographical location, issue, or piece of legislation (King et al. 1994: 4), with a view to discerning patterns, trends and relationships between key variables. The 'language' of qualitative research tends to revolve around case-studies and social contexts instead of 'variables' and 'hypotheses', although, of course, some people use all of these terms.

This type of research involves the interpretation of data, whereby the researcher analyses cases, usually a few in number, in their social and cultural context over a specific period of time, and may develop grounded theories (see chapter 6 for more on this) that emphasise tracing the process and sequence of events in specific settings (see Holloway 1997: 80–7). Hence, in contrast to quantitative research, the researcher is not detached from, but positively interacts with, the object of study. Critics of this type of research point out that studies are usually small-scale and not generalisable beyond the case researched.

Qualitative research has enabled complementary research into such topics as the nature of dictatorships, by interviewing people who lived under such conditions and by uncovering the 'texture' of the relationship between the state and its citizens. It is unlikely that such 'rich' findings would be produced by statistical data alone. The aim for the new researcher is to weigh up and choose the best combination of possible methods to shed the maximum light on her chosen topic.

Ethnographic studies are generally qualitative in nature, for this type of enquiry usually requires the researcher to submerge herself in the culture of a given society or group with the aim of finding patterns of power between specific group members, studying symbols of identity formation, and so on. Such a study usually entails a prolonged period of actually living in and among the group under observation, often befriending them and becoming part of their community. A full-blown ethnographic study is not always practical, given the time constraints of modern-day studies. The human sciences are, however, full of in-depth case-studies, which draw on many ethnographic research methods, whereby researchers spend up to one-third of their total research time undertaking work in the field. Another type of qualitative enquiry is sometimes called **thick description** (Geertz 1973). Here, social phenomena are traced back to their origins in detail, by reconstructing specific events and using a wide variety of sources – which in some cases may be cross-checked with one another, or **triangulated** – to arrive at a plausible 'description' of the chosen subject of study (the notion of triangulation in research is discussed below).

Box 38 Criticisms of qualitative research at a glance

Some of the common and recurring criticisms of qualitative research tend to be the following:

- There is a perceived problem of 'anecdotalism'; that is, the use of brief or limited examples in relation to explanations. For critics, this tends to raise questions about the representativeness and generality of the piece of research.
- This inability to generalise from small samples or few cases leads to a question of the validity of results based on such research.
- The 'immersion' of the researcher in the social context she is studying leads to a lack of 'objectivity' and a propensity to use personal opinion instead of evidence to support arguments.

▶ The quantitative–qualitative dichotomy: A false antithesis

There are a number of issues in the human sciences that revolve around the quantitative–qualitative dichotomy. Table 8 does *not* seek to underline or subscribe to this dichotomy but rather shows *how* both types of research are often perceived among academics.

Table 8 THE SO-CALLED QUANTITATIVE–QUALITATIVE DICHOTOMY

Quantitative	Qualitative
• interested in finding out numerical qualities of an event or case: how many, how much?	• interested in the nature and essence of an event, person or case
• goal of investigation is prediction, control, description, hypothesis-testing	• goal of investigation is understanding, description, discovery, hypothesis-generation
• uses hard data (numbers)	• soft data (words or images from documents or observations, etc.)
• objective	• subjective
• usually tackles macro-issues, using large, random and representative samples	• tends to analyse micro-issues, using small, non-random and non-representative samples
• employs a deductive research strategy	• employs an inductive research strategy
• its epistemological orientation is argued to be rooted in the positivist tradition	• its epistemological orientation is argued to be rooted in the interpretative tradition
• aims at identifying general patterns and relationships	• aims at interpreting events of historical and cultural significance
• measures are created prior to data collection and are standardised	• measures are created during interaction with data and are often specific to the individual setting
• survey methodology	• interview (in-depth case-study)
• procedures are standard, replication is presumed	• research procedures are particular, replication rare
• value-free	• political
• abstract	• grounded
• concepts are in the form of variables	• concepts are in the form of themes and motifs
• findings attempt to be comprehensive, holistic and generalisable	• findings are seen to be precise, narrow and not generalisable

Source: · Adapted from Mason 1998: 27–8; Silverman 2000: 2; Neuman 2000: 123; Danermark et al. 2002: 162.

Table 8 broadly sets out how both strands of research have come to be associated with certain types of enquiry in academia. There is no reason why one should not employ methods usually associated with quantitative research in an in-depth case-study of a particular town, for example undertaking a statistical analysis of variables pertaining to people's voting habits, their socio-economic status and choice of newspaper. Equally, methods usually associated with qualitative research are frequently employed in comparative analyses across cases, for example using the interview technique to speak to political élites in a number of countries.

Box 39   Methods – quantitative or qualitative?

We need to distinguish between quantitative and qualitative research strategies, in which the emphasis is on quantitative *and* qualitative research respectively and quantitative and qualitative methods. Some methods clearly lend themselves to either quantitative or qualitative analysis (see below); however, most methods can be used in both, so a neat division between them does not reflect their real use and value. Consider the following: interviews, commonly associated with qualitative research, can be 'structured and analysed in a quantitative manner' (and, as we shall see below, they often are) and surveys, usually associated with quantitative research, 'may allow for open-ended responses and lead to the in-depth study of individual cases', or, in other words, a qualitative approach (Blaxter et al. 1997: 610).

Examples of methods associated with quantitative research:
- questionnaire or survey technique
- 'structured observation' (predetermined schedule)
- content analysis (predetermined categories).

Examples of methods associated with qualitative research:
- interview/oral history
- observation (participant/non-participant)
- documentary analysis.

As we shall see below, methods can be mixed and, indeed, in many cases ought to be. The point of table 8 is simply to flag up some of the different terms associated with the broad division in methods. In reality, this division is to some extent artificial, and the best research usually employs both methods (King et al. 1994: 5). The key for new researchers is not to become entrenched in one camp or the other, a sentiment I hinted at when discussing disciplinary boundaries in chapter 5. Hammersley, with whom many academics may not fully agree, neatly sums this up when he states that 'the process of inquiry in sciences is the same whatever method is used, and the retreat into paradigms effectively stultifies debate and hampers progress' (1992: 182, cited in Silverman 2000: 11). This is true to a certain extent. However, it must be said that academics with competing ontological and epistemological views would have problems with a universal 'process of inquiry' and may not believe 'progress' to be possible in the human sciences in the first place.

Box 40   The question–method fit

You should choose your methods according to the questions you wish to ask. Whatever method you employ in your studies, you need to bear in mind that 'methods should follow from questions' (Punch 2000a: 5), not the other way around. A poor question–method fit can lead to serious delays in research and, ultimately undermine your project. There are two key reasons for spending some time considering the question–method fit in your work. The first is that the questions you wish to ask should, to a great extent, guide your choice of methods. This is a logical research step that points you to a specific method of obtaining information. You will need to decide, after an extensive literature review (see chapter 3), which is the most appropriate method for your project and why the other methods used by the scholars you have read are not more suitable. Secondly, as Punch explains, by starting with the research question, you avoid what he terms '*methodolatry*, a combination of *method* and *idolatry* to describe a preoccupation with selecting and defending methods to the exclusion of the actual substance of the story being told' (ibid.: 21). You need to bear in mind that methods are only tools with which researchers obtain information – unless, of course, your thesis is concerned with the nature of methods themselves.

Both the quantitative and qualitative paradigms, and the methods associated with them, have as their goal the making of inferences: that is, 'using facts we know to learn something about facts we do not know' (King et al. 1994: 119). Whatever the method, the researcher needs to guard against misusing them. Ultimately, any method of enquiry in research can be manipulated (which amounts to cheating) to produce different results from those that the researcher would have had with the **data** he or she really collected. It is not for nothing that Disraeli once stated, 'There are lies, damned lies and statistics.' Equally, imprecise details of interview partners and interview techniques, and of their relevance to the study, constitute bad scholarship. Manipulating information derived from interviews, especially those that are not recorded, or from any form of **data collection**, is dishonest and deceitful, but that will not prevent it from taking place. No one method is better than any other, but some methods are more relevant to your project than others. As I suggest below, one way of avoiding false conclusions drawn from empirical data is to have more than one method of enquiry.

▶ Methods

Introducing methods of enquiry

This section highlights some of the most common research methods used in gathering and analysing empirical data *in the field* and comments on their key characteristics. In addition, there follows a brief introduction to questionnaires, because they are frequently employed alongside interviews and in some cases produce very similar data. This is not an exhaustive list of the myriad methods on offer and you are advised to consult a book on research methods for further, and more specific, information relevant to each method, in particular statistical analyses, as these are very specialised, and an in-depth text should be consulted before adopting them (for example, see Pennings et al. 1999). The point here is briefly to introduce methods common to many advanced undergraduate and postgraduate studies, namely different types of interview techniques, questionnaires, participant and non-participant observation, and certain types of documentary analysis. The list below is not presented in order of preference, complexity or usefulness. You need to think carefully through your research questions before selecting a method with which to seek to answer them. The short description of methods in this book is intended to assist in this process.

Although humanities students may not use the terms employed in this section, they do use, directly or indirectly, many of the methods outlined below. It may not be possible to interview Goethe and ask him his opinion on certain matters, but it may be possible to interview a Goethe specialist and gather information in this way. In any case, the discussion below is not discipline-specific and is relevant to researchers who intend using any of the methods discussed.

Interview technique

The interview is a very popular method among students, especially élite interviewing, and for this reason more space is given over to it. Four broad types of interview technique can be used: the structured, the semi-structured and the unstructured interview, and group interviews (or focus groups, as they are sometimes called). Interview data can be collected either quantitatively (except for unstructured interviews) or qualitatively. Before introducing the interview method, some general points should be made:

1 It is usually wise *not* to use interviews as the *sole* method in your study, but rather to apply them in conjunction with other methods of enquiry. Looking at the same phenomena from different angles will ensure a more balanced approach to your object of study and will probably shed more light on it (see 'triangulation of methods' below).

2 Is interviewing really for you? Are you the right type of person to be interviewing? If the thought of meeting (important) strangers fills you with dread and brings you out in a cold sweat, then this is probably the wrong method to choose, though this will clearly have implications for your project's topic and research questions.

3 The biggest problem students have with interviews is access to individuals, companies or institutions. This is something that needs to be thought about as soon as possible after beginning your studies. Writing to, and receiving a reply from, prospective interviewees can be a very lengthy business, something to factor into your research plans.

4 Find out exactly how much time the interviewees will have for you, so you can arrange the interview accordingly.

5 Always give yourself plenty of time to get to where you are going, as you certainly do not wish to keep people – usually very busy people – waiting, and you do not want to arrive at the interview sweating and out of breath. Make sure you have done your homework and found out where the interview is actually taking place (Grant 2000: 7).

6 Make sure you have the correct equipment with you (including more than one pen) and that you are very familiar with your recording apparatus, as you and your interviewee do not want to waste time at the beginning of the interview fumbling about with equipment. If you are recording the interview (which, of course, you ask and obtain explicit permission to do) the best piece of equipment to use for perfect sound quality is a mini-disc recorder. Otherwise a good quality dictaphone will suffice. Whether to record interviews or not is a decision you need to consider. Interviewees tend to be more open and specific off the record, but this makes referencing the source and recording the interview somewhat more difficult.

7 Listen to and analyse your recording(s) or notes as soon as possible after the interview, in order to get the clearest picture possible of what has been said and have the best chance of clarifying any

omissions in your notes 'while the interview is still fresh in your mind' (ibid.: 14).

Structured interviews

The structured interview, as its name suggests, is the most rigorous and the least flexible in the way it is set up. Predetermined questions are put to the interviewee in a specific order and the responses are logged (either by recording electronically or by note-taking). The same process is repeated with a number of other interviewees and the results or findings can be compared with one another, categorised according to specific questions, and aggregated statistically. Usually, interviews are carried out by the researcher, face-to-face with her interviewee. However, the structured technique can be also carried out via e-mail or by telephone (Kumar 1999: 109). In this situation, interviewees receive the same prompt from the interviewer and there is not a great deal of digression from the script or interview schedule. The questions asked are usually 'closed', i.e. the interviewee has only a fixed number of answers, and data resulting from the answers can be coded and processed easily (Bryman 2001: 107–8). This technique is very close to survey questionnaires on which answers to predetermined questions are written in specific sections instead of given orally. The key aim of structured interviews is to achieve a high degree of standardisation or uniformity, and hence ease of comparability, in the format of the answers. The drawback is that this technique is inflexible and is not designed to cope with the unexpected. On the plus side, you need fewer interviewing skills than are necessary for the unstructured interview – and even the semi-structured one – because in this situation you have a 'map' to guide you – a fairly rigidly drafted question sheet. It is this device that ensures a relatively uniform delivery of questions and prompts. On the negative side, you may miss the opportunity of discovering important information, owing to the inflexible nature of this type of interview.

Semi-structured and unstructured interviews

One step down from the structured interview is the semi-structured, or in-depth, interview, in which you, the interviewer, have in mind a number of questions (you should not exceed ten in total, for manageability) that you wish to put to interviewees, but which do not have to follow any specific, predetermined order. The advantage of this, perhaps the most popular method of interviewing, is that it allows a certain degree of flexibility and allows for the pursuit of unexpected lines of enquiry during the interview. The results and findings of such an interview can still be compared, contrasted and even converted into statistics. An unstructured interview, on the other hand, is one in which the researcher has a random list of concepts or loose questions, which he or she converts into spontaneous questions during the interview. Another, relatively popular, version of this is the so-called 'oral-history' interview, in which open-ended questions are put to interviewees, who are actively encouraged to talk about their own biographies and to 'recount aspects of their lives and/or the lives of their contemporaries' (Blaikie 2000: 234). This technique can be helpful at the very beginning of a project, as unstructured sessions can open up avenues of investigation, including informal discussions, previously unthought of. However, the answers and data gathered from such sessions are not comparable, as the content of each interview is likely to be very different.

Group interviews or focus groups

Group interviews usually involve the researcher and a specific group of people, for example from a particular age cohort (youths), socio-economic background (the working class) or ethnic background. This type of interview can also be structured, semi-structured or unstructured and recorded in the same ways as one-to-one interviews, that is, either quantitatively or qualitatively. Your role as researcher is, however, different in as much as you now act as a 'moderator or facilitator, and less of an interviewer' (Punch 2000b: 177). The idea is to spark a dialogue between group members guided by topics supplied by you, and not to hold a traditional interview on a one-to-one basis.

Interviewing has many advantages, especially if you are aware of the pitfalls of relying solely on the data produced from them. They can provide information that is not printed or recorded elsewhere, and interviewees can assist in interpreting complex documents, decisions or policies. Also, interviewees, especially at the élite level, can provide you with further contacts. This is sometimes called the 'snowball' technique (Grant 2000: 3), whereby you ask, specifically, whether the interviewee could name any useful contacts, thus allowing you to get in touch with important people using the interviewee's name and without having to resort to 'cold calling'.

Questionnaire

Questionnaires are most effective when used in conjunction with other methods, especially one or more varieties of the interview technique. Put simply, a questionnaire is a list of questions sent to specific individuals, who then, if you are lucky, respond. It is vital that questions be clear, unambiguous and easy to understand (Kumar 1999: 110). If a respondent misunderstands a question only slightly, her reply is very likely to be of little value to you and she is less likely to respond in the first place. If a number of your respondents understand a question differently from each other, their answers will be difficult to compare with one another. Remember, unlike in a face-to-face interview, you will not be at hand to explain anything to the respondent, who must rely on the information in front of her. This may be an advantage, as there will be no 'interviewer effects' on the answers; that is, your personal characteristics (socio-economic background, gender, etc.) will not affect the respondent's answers (Bryman 2001: 130). Try to avoid leading questions, or questions which tend to leave only one option open to respondents. Questions on sensitive matters should be preceded by a brief summary, 'explaining the relevance of the question' to the study (ibid.), and giving the respondent some context to it. The questions should follow each other in a logical order (you should take great care to avoid unintentional duplication and arrange questions in the correct sequence) and should be set out in a user-friendly manner. This type of method requires careful consideration and is best undertaken only after you have developed a matured and very clear, precise idea of what it is you want to study. If you do decide to employ this method, you must consult a relevant textbook, attend a proper course or, pref- erably, both.

A good way of combining questionnaires with interviews is to have a separate question on the questionnaire sheet asking if respondents would be prepared to be interviewed at a later date. In this way you will have access to, and be able to mix, quantitative and qualitative data.

The response rate of questionnaires will differ widely. The obvious aim is to get back as many as possible. However, there is a general methodological problem here, as it is likely that those who do not respond to your questionnaire are different to, or hold different views to, those who do. As long as you are aware of this potential bias, you can use other methods and data to correct it.

The observation technique

There are two basic types of observation technique: participant and non-participant. The first of these has been touched upon above, with reference to (predominantly qualitative) ethnographic studies. This is the chief technique of data collection for ethnographers and anthropologists, who submerge themselves in the culture, customs, norms and practices of the people they are studying. One of the aims of actually being among the subjects of investigation is to understand how everyday life is conducted (Punch 2000b: 184) by discerning specific patterns of behaviour, gestures, use of language, symbols and tradition.

Many researchers will use some form of direct observation, not necessarily as intense as that described above. By noting down and categorising what you observe, you are recording snapshots of empirical phenomena. For example, you may take part in a form of direct political action like a social movement or demonstration. In explaining how such an event came to take place you would need to draw on other works analysing the factors that motivate participation in the first place, as being present at an event does not guarantee you will gain a clear understanding of this. Again, as long as you remain aware of the pitfalls of extrapolating from unique incidents, and as long as you link your findings to the wider literature on this subject, such direct observation of unfolding events can prove invaluable. However, for exciting revolutions and political coups, you are unlikely to be in the right place at the right time. Seriously, securing access to observe people, groups, etc., can be difficult, and even if you do gain access, you need to ensure that your presence does not unduly affect the action of others in their 'natural setting'. Some researchers structure their observations much in the same way as an interviewer does in a structured interview. They have a notion of what they should be looking for and how they should record the findings. The findings can be used for quantitative analysis, similarly to the data produced by structured interviews.

Non-participant observation usually involves a passive role for the researcher, who does not directly influence events, but observes interaction, which, it is assumed, is unaffected by the researcher's presence. For example, a researcher may observe the interaction between a child and its mother or a group of children playing, taking notes or even videotaping the scene (on how to take fieldwork notes, see Neuman 2000: 363–6). Videotaping gives you the option of going over and over the 'original' data, analysing modes of interaction (Blaikie 2000: 233–4).

In the literature on research methods there is a general distinction between structured and unstructured observation, which centres on the issue of either going into the field with particular categories, concepts or classifications in mind or not. Unstructured observation is characterised as an approach out of which classificatory systems and patterns emerge. As with many components of research, you can, of course, combine the two by starting with loose categories which you adapt in the light of unstructured observation. This distinction, and the possible combination, is not unlike the discussion of inductive and deductive theory in chapter 6. The debate is about the extent to which the researcher inter-acts with empirical data, applying or modifying preconceived concepts, notions, expectations and assumptions. There is a thin line between using conceptual tools as a means of guidance and being over-reliant on them, ending up with tunnel vision, and failing to notice or deal adequately with phenomena outside the reach of the conceptual tools used.

Documentary analysis
Documentary evidence comes in all shapes and sizes, ranging from official and private documents to personal letters or memos. To some extent all theses engage with specific texts or documents. The level at which this is done can range from the full-blown and technical discourse analysis to simply reading texts with the aim of gaining information of a person's or organisation's viewpoint or policy. This type of analysis will point you to very specific sources, in this case written documents or texts. You must consider carefully the origins and authors of these documents or texts, the purpose they were originally written for, and the audience they were intended to address. In addition, you have to distinguish between *primary* and *secondary* document sources, with the former usually considered those that have arisen as a product of the actual research process and the latter as interpretations of events by others (Bell 1993: 68). For example, if you record and transcribe your interviews, these could be considered primary sources. If, on the other hand, a second researcher uses your transcriptions for her research, she would be using secondary sources. This is not a very good idea in reality, given that they were not present at the original interview and are thus analysing the record of a conversation. That record has been recorded and interpreted (from tape to text) by you. The results can be manipulated statistically or interpreted qualitatively, or both.

The archival technique
Archives vary a great deal across a wide range of different source materials. However, a few general points can be made about using this method. First, as with interviews, you need to secure access at a very early stage in the research process; for example, in Germany there is a waiting list of approximately one year to view the files of the former secret police (the 'Stasi'). This has obvious implications for you as a student who, at a relatively early stage, needs to have thought through and decided upon exactly which archival files you intend to use. The next step is to contact the archive in question and arrange dates when you can visit. A good idea, if possible, is to make an exploratory visit

or, better still, a thorough reading of the archive's website, checking the content of the archive (scouring the indexes of files) narrowing down and selecting the material you wish to order. The guides, catalogues, referencing systems and rules on photocopying vary tremendously from archive to archive (see Vickers 1997: 174).

Archival sources are to be looked upon as 'primary' sources and unearthing such sources and employing them in a research project offers an excellent source-base with which to launch a study. The chief aim of using this type of method is to bring 'dead' documents alive to shed light on specific events, personalities or policies by introducing them to a wider readership. You must take care, as with all data gathered, not simply to select the documents or files that support your hypotheses, for the latter may be *refuted* and not just verified.

Finally, a word or two on the archivists working in the archives. In many historical archives, especially in Europe, an archivist may be assigned to you. The role of the archivist is not to be underestimated, and it can be a matter of luck whether or not you end up with one who is sufficiently interested in your project. But luck can be given a helping hand by courteous and professional treatment of archivists – at a minimum, punctuality and acknowledgement of assistance is essential. There seems to be a relationship between the interest an archivist shows in your project and the type, amount and quality of data you will receive. Under normal circumstances you should obtain most of the standard documents listed in a catalogue. If, however, you chance upon a keen archivist, you may be lucky to find that there are many relevant files that are not listed in the sections that you have been wading through.

In larger archives, for example, the Public Records Office in the UK, it is very unlikely that you will have an archivist assigned to you, so you need to do your homework thoroughly beforehand. There is no reason why the results of archival work, once again, cannot be used, recorded and presented either qualitatively or quantitatively, or both.

Documents

All documents have been written with a purpose in mind, are based on particular assumptions and are presented in a certain way or style. A political party's manifesto or regular documents for dissemination are a case in point. A trade union will also have a particular angle on events, as will a think-tank or an association linked to a political ideology. The researcher must be fully aware of the *origins*, *purpose* and original *audience* of any document before researching it. In this way you can analyse the documents in the context in which they were written. This method of data analysis is often linked to **hermeneutics**, an approach which seeks to analyse a text from the perspective of the person who penned it, whilst emphasising the social and historical context within which it was produced (Bryman 2001: 382–3). For example, an internal memo from one level of government to another in a dictatorship may shed light on how the centre maintains power and the way in which information feeds back into the system of control. This document may, on the other hand, say more about the individual sending it than the system as a whole. Other documents may have been phrased in a certain way to appease superiors, when in fact what they were reporting was a distortion of the truth, as was the case with the official 'feedback' mechanisms (i.e. the secret police) in many former communist countries. The best guard against biased findings is to use other methods or sources to complement the documents you have collected.

Documents made public which clearly state a party's, association's or organisation's aims and objectives can be used as a very good benchmark against which you can measure on-the-ground reality. A housing association, for example, may state that its central concern is investment in social housing to empower local residents to engage in local activities directly related to where and how people live. You might analyse these documents and perhaps speak to a few key individuals in the association and build up a succinct list of their intended aims. Now you have a resource from which you can construct a questionnaire or interview questions to 'check' against reality in fieldwork. If the association's aims and objectives can be measured statistically – for example, crime rates, attacks, and so on – this could be used to complement the above techniques of data collection.

Discourse analysis
A more sophisticated form of document analysis is discourse analysis. This technique, increasingly borrowed by the social sciences from linguistics, studies the shifts and turns in the use of language over time or in particular usage, often in the form of a microanalysis, for example where the researcher identifies active and passive verbs, and so on. Social scientists have discovered this technique and are employing it to get at such tricky or 'slippery' concepts as identity. For example, social constructivists in the field of international relations, leaning on work undertaken in sociology, draw on discourse analysis to understand the way in which identities, ideas and institutions interact with and impact on each other. At its most complex, this type of analysis uses

special software packages to deduce patterns and changes in language use by examining, electronically, a database or corpus capable of storing millions of words. The latter can be described as 'The collection of computer-readable language that you assemble for your project selected on the basis of your research criteria' (Barnbrook, cited in Hoffman and Knowles 1999: 28).

Print media

Print media, especially newspaper articles and reports, are a popular source in students' projects. They can be a useful complement to interviews and statistics. If you are undertaking an historical study, newspaper reports can give you a 'feel' for the views and opinions of the printed press, or the wider opinions they represented at that time. A more up-to-date study may indicate and inform you of wider sentiments in the country you are studying – for example, British and American attitudes towards the war in Iraq. You need to be fully aware that the media landscape is very broad and represents a wide range of diverse interests. Thus a comparative analysis of *The Sun* in England and *The New York Times* in America with respect to the Iraq war may not give you a comprehensive and nuanced account of the advantages and disadvantages of military action. Therefore try, as far as possible, to alleviate obvious bias by using two or three newspapers with different political allegiances. It is particularly important for a researcher working in a foreign country to be fully informed of, and knowledgeable about, that country's print media to be able to make, and ultimately justify, their choice of newspaper sources.

Print media can be a useful source for academic research, and most organisations and political parties produce something in written form. If you intend to analyse the content of media in a systematic and comprehensive manner, you may wish to employ a quantitative analysis of reporting in one specific newspaper over a certain period of time. This type of 'content analysis' uses predetermined categories, but is not, as is often suggested, in opposition to more 'qualitative' approaches. Rather, it should be seen as a complementary method by which to collect data. Alternatively, a qualitative approach might mean having to find out who compiles the reports or articles, who is the target audience and under what conditions they were written, as a Chinese 'underground' newsletter is likely to be written in a different style to, say, *The Times*. Interestingly, in analyses of newspapers, for example, one can discover certain patterns or emphases of reporting on particular topics, or indeed a change in topics and themes themselves over a period of time. This can be carried out in either a quantitative or qualitative research strategy. With the introduction of CD-ROMs, researching back-copies of newspaper editions has become much easier. You can now type in keywords, for example 'unemployment', and retrieve all articles in the past year or more on the topic, count them, download them, organise them into categories and begin the analysis. This is an excellent way to get a quick overview at the beginning of your studies.

You do need to be aware, however, that you must not rely too heavily on quotes from newspapers to support your dissertation or thesis, as this will not impress the examiners and may point to the fact that you have no other sources to back up your assertions.

▶ Triangulation, mixing methods and data

We now have an idea of some of the most common research methods used in undergraduate and postgraduate dissertations and theses. Generally, it is a good idea to try and use more than one method of enquiry to improve your chances of getting better, more reliable data, and to minimise the chance of biased findings. Using more than one method in research is sometimes referred to as triangulation, but it is not as simple as it first sounds. This term is derived from navigation, military strategy and surveying, which, according to Blaikie (2000: 263–70), is misleading and has led to the popular conception that triangulation simply means approaching an object of study from different angles using different methods. He points out that triangulation is, in fact, very difficult, chiefly because of the different ontological and epistemological underpinnings of research strategies, consisting of combinations of methods, which are used. Many scholars point to this difficulty in combining research methods. Here I re-emphasise that methods themselves should be viewed as mere tools for collecting data. They should not be looked upon as being automatically 'rooted in epistemological and ontological commitments' (Bryman 2001: 445), even though (some) academics and their disciplines often forcibly uphold the notion that certain methods are inextricably bound up with specific world-views. In other words, as long as you are aware of *how* you are employing a specific method and *what* this method is pointing you towards, and *how* this relates to the ways in which you employ other methods, there should be no problem. The key point is to check whether your methods are ontologically consistent with one another, and, as a consequence, whether they are epistemologically consistent (see box 41).

Box 41   Mixing methods and data

Mason alerts us to the limitations of triangulation by asking:

Are you, for example, seeking to corroborate one source and method with another, or enhance validity and reliability through some form of triangulation of method? If you are doing this, you will need to think about on what basis one set of data, or one method, can corroborate another. This will involve asking whether the two sets of data tell you about the same phenomena, or whether the two methods yield comparable data. Often they do not, and you cannot therefore expect straightforward corroboration. (Mason 1998: 25–6)

When speaking about triangulation in research, it is important to differentiate between a number of factors that can be triangulated. Method triangulation is a process in which the researcher uses two or more research methods to investigate the same phenomenon. This can be done either sequentially, that is, one method after the other, or at the same time. In most studies it is not possible to use more than one method at a time, so that a sequence of stages of research emerges. It is among these stages, and the various methods used, that checks and balances between data can be made. For example, you might first undertake in-depth qualitative interviews and follow this up with a questionnaire that could be used for statistical analysis (see Neuman 2000: 125).

On the other hand, data triangulation is a process in which the researcher uses multiple sources of data, a process similar to that used in some comparative analyses where the same object of study is analysed using a number of different measures or variables (Peters 1998: 97). An example of cross-checking data which have been collected using different methods is the comparison of interview transcripts with published documents, or statistics derived from a local investigation which are compared with other national, statistical sources for accuracy (see Robins 1995: 72).

If we disregard the semantics of the word 'triangulation' and concentrate on what it has come to mean in the human sciences, the best summary would simply be that it *is* about observing an object of study from different angles. The major benefit for the researcher, and scholarship in general, is that findings or conclusions are 'likely to be much more convincing and accurate if ... based on several different sources of information' (Yin 1994: 92). Thus, the best advice to you is to attempt to check findings derived from one type of method with those derived from another, as long as the original fact under investigation *remains the same*, thereby enhancing the validity of your study. However, beware of falling into the trap of using various methods superficially, skipping between methods because one does not seem to bear the results you were hoping for (see Silverman 2000: 99).

▶ Summary

- Methods should be chosen for their appropriateness in answering the questions posed (remember the 'question–method' match).
- Most of the methods discussed briefly above can be used in quantitative *and* qualitative research strategies.
- Try not to employ just *one* method of data collection, but attempt to mix methods and data to add to your project's validity (often called 'triangulation' of methods or data).

▶ Essential reading

Marsh, D. and Stoker, G. (eds) (2002) *Theory and Methods in Political Science*, Basingstoke, Palgrave Macmillan, 2nd edn, chapters 9, 10 and 11.
Mason, J. (1996) *Qualitative Researching*, London, Sage, chapters 1, 2 and 8.
Neuman, W. L. (2000) *Social Research Methods. Qualitative and Quantitative Approaches*, Boston, MA, Allyn & Bacon, 4th edn, chapters 6, 7 and 8.
Punch, K. F. (2000b) *Introduction to Social Research. Quantitative and Qualitative Approaches*, London, Thousand Oaks, CA and New Delhi: Sage, especially chapters 5 and 8.

▶ Further reading

Bryman, A. (2001) *Social Research Methods*, Oxford, Oxford University Press.
Kumar, R. (1999) *Research Methodology. A Step-By-Step Guide for Beginners*, London, Thousand Oaks, CA and New Delhi, Sage.
Ragin, C. C. (1994) *Constructing Social Research. The Unity and Diversity of Method*, Thousand Oaks, CA, Pine Forge Press, chapters 4 and 6.
Silverman, D. (2000) *Doing Qualitative Research. A Practical Handbook*, London, Thousand Oaks, CA and New Delhi, Sage.

8 Academic Standards, Plagiarism and Ethics in Research

Chapter 8 offers a discussion of plagiarism and ethics in research. It does so by:

• Introducing the concepts of academic standards and plagiarism
• Warning against sloppy referencing in your projects
• Introducing ethics in social research
• Introducing a continuum of ethics along which certain types of research can be placed

▶ Why worry about academic standards, plagiarism and ethics?

You may be forgiven for wondering why we need to discuss academic standards, plagiarism and ethics in a book about the foundations of research. Well, the first and most obvious reason is that students and scholars alike need to reflect on such crucial topics *prior* to undertaking their projects, as the answers to many of the questions they raise will determine how and what they research.

In order to implement the lessons we have learnt from the previous seven chapters, we need – as researchers and students – to conduct our work within acceptable academic standards. The basis of such good practice is sound referencing (see below for a special section on referencing) and a reflection on the ethics of our research. One of the major flip-sides to proper academic standards is plagiarism, which has taken on a new importance in an era of widespread internet accessibility, offering new opportunities for conducting research and gathering knowledge, but also for cheating (although there is software available to track down cheats). Below I set out to describe the concept of plagiarism and also offer some concrete advice on how to avoid sloppy scholarship and hence accusations of plagiarism.

Increasingly we need to be aware of the importance of ethics in our research. Ethics is not a watertight science and can be, as we shall see, open to some interpretation. However, my task is simply to acquaint you with an outline of the key debates on this topic, the language they are carried out in, and offer examples of research for you to reflect on. Beyond flagging up some of the key issues at stake regarding ethics and social research, there is nothing 'prescriptive' in the overview below. As you will soon see, one person's idea of ethical behaviour is another's breach of trust. There is no cut-and-dried right or wrong answer in the way in which we choose to conduct certain aspects of our research (except with regards to plagiarism), but there are generally acceptable and unacceptable codes of conduct we need to be aware of.

Plagiarism

Plagiarism is a well-known term, but an extremely hard one to define in practice. The original meaning of the term was 'kidnapping', although it has now come to mean the act of stealing *or presenting as one's own* the ideas, utterances or work of someone else.

Plagiarism is a serious business in academia, from first degrees right through to doctorates. For this reason, make sure that you obtain your institution's guidelines on plagiarism at the earliest possible opportunity. The following discussion draws heavily on Ben Rosamond's illuminating article (2002: 167–9), in which he rightly points out the differences in definitions of this term and goes on to establish exactly what constitutes an act of plagiarism. Furthermore, Rosamond outlines four ways in which plagiarism is generally understood:

1 Plagiarism reflects shoddy scholarship and the failure to meet the exacting standards expected in academic life: 'Discovered or latent, intended or "accidental", an act of plagiarism reflects badly on the perpetrator and casts serious doubts on his or her credibility as a scholar or as a student worthy of a university-level education' (Rosamond 2002: 168).
2 Plagiarism is seen as an infringement of the informal practices that allow academic life to proceed; that is, a breakdown of trust between teacher and student, and among students themselves.

3 A further approach is to see the act of plagiarism as actually breaching ethical codes and standards.
4 The final way of looking at plagiarism is to see it in legal terms of a breach of copyright and a form of fraud. This includes the violation of the intellectual property of an original author of the piece of work plagiarised. Akin to this is the notion of 'stealing' people's ideas and passing them off as your own, effectively reaping what you did not sow.

The explosion of web-based activities has boosted the potential for plagiarism to an extent that is very difficult to estimate. With websites specifically focusing on offering academic essays which can be purchased by credit card, the chances of cheating have greatly increased, while the chances of catching blatant cheats are becoming slimmer. The fact that students at undergraduate and taught-graduate level routinely prepare their essays on computers and submit them electronically has, ironically, meant that it is relatively easy to check for cheats by using search engines. To avoid any misunderstandings make sure that you cite the exact website and date if you use any material from the web.

As Rosamond rightly points out, the temptation to cheat is usually greater as deadlines loom and funding dries up. Learn good time-management skills from the start and avoid including anything in your thesis that you cannot honestly account for. There is an increasing need to protect yourself against accusations of plagiarism, especially in the light of strict ownership of data, copyright and intellectual property rights laws. The following section offers some tips on how to avoid sloppy scholarship and accusations of plagiarism.

Referencing – keeping academic standards

It is a very good idea to start proper referencing and a bibliography from the outset of your project, and to decide on the type of referencing system you wish to use (Harvard or Humanities) and stick with it throughout the text. Proper referencing includes noting down accurate records of page numbers, the book, journal or newspaper title, the author and, most easily overlooked and forgotten, the place, publisher and publication date of the source you are citing from (see Table 9 below for examples of referencing). If you are photocopying from a book or journal, you should also photocopy the title page and the imprints page – the one with all the crucial details on it, usually on the reverse of the title page. Taking care in recording accurate notes will save you an inordinate amount of time (in the time some people spend

Table 9 REFERENCING: THE 'HARVARD' AND 'HUMANITIES' METHODS OF REFERENCING

This, perhaps the most commonly used system in journals, is an easy and efficient way of referencing your sources. In the text you cite the author's name, the year of publication and, if you are referring to a specific passage or quotation, the page number. This is placed in brackets in the text: (Cooke 2000: 43). In the bibliography or reference list, give the full bibliographical details of the text: that is, the author's name and initial, year of publication, book or article title, place of publication (usually a town) and publisher. For example:

Cooke, P. (2000) *Speaking the Taboo: A Study of the Work of Wolfgang Hilbig*, Amsterdam and Atlanta, Rodopi.

A note for purists: to be precise, the 'Harvard' system is just one example of a *name–date system*. However, the specific term has now almost completely displaced the general, as with 'Hoover' and 'vacuum cleaner'. As you purists will already know, this is called synecdoche.

The 'Humanities' or 'numeric' method of referencing

The 'Humanities' method of referencing involves the citation of references by a superscript numeral in the text, with the full bibliographical details of the work given in the footnote text at the bottom of the page or in endnotes at the end of the section or chapter. The same information as in the example above needs to be given.

Whichever system you choose, keep with it throughout the whole text (see Fairbairn and Winch 2000: 116–25 for a full discussion of referencing).

on searching for lost citations and references they could have written another chapter or article). Good and careful note-taking is closely linked to the notion of academic honesty and the avoidance of plagiarism (see Rosamond 2002: 172–3). The latter is looked upon as the crime of all crimes in academia and will see you fail the particular essay you are writing, get you excluded from your university and, for a doctorate, probably result in you being blacklisted in the academic community.

It can also lead to litigation. I therefore reiterate the need to get into the habit of comprehensively recording bibliographical details of all the reading you undertake, as you will forget the precise reference quite quickly, which may become a problem if you, or someone else, discovers at a later date that an apparently unrelated article is actually germane to your project.

Whatever referencing system you use, you must be careful not to mix practices together, by using endnotes, footnotes and references in the main text. You can, however, use both references and footnotes, with the latter providing additional information other than on the sources used. Your choice of referencing system, again, may be governed by your department's regulations, so it is best to check, as wasted hours can be spent reformatting footnotes to endnotes and vice versa. Many a student – and senior academic too – has spent several weeks at the end of her studies scrambling around redoing footnotes or endnotes that were left behind unfinished in a creative burst of intellectual activity somewhere in year one. Remember from day one to keep an accurate note of all the books and articles you have read or cited in a bibliographical list. As soon as you find something new, get into the habit of adding it to the list immediately.

▶ Ethics in research

Ethics impact on all forms of social research. A researcher has a set of moral principles that guide her in the choice of how to conduct herself with regard to such topics as confidentiality, anonymity, legality, professionalism and privacy when dealing with people in research (Blaxter et al. 1997: 148). As a researcher you have a duty to respect the people you are studying and you need to make sure you ask their explicit permission first, and then make very clear how you intend to collect, analyse and disseminate the data you have gathered by talking to them.

Box 42   What are ethics?

Denscombe nicely sums up the role of ethics in research thus:

At a practical level, it deals with what *ought* to be done and what ought not to be done. The word 'ought' recurs time and again when ethics comes into considerations and, for researchers, this calls for some change in their approach to the process of research. The problem is no longer one of what it is possible or logical to do, crucial to the rest of the research methodology, but one of what ought to be done taking into consideration the rules of conduct that indicate what it is right and proper to do. It calls for a moral perspective on things, rather than a practical perspective. (2002: 175)

Turn to our trusty dictionary – that hasn't actually helped us much as yet – and under 'ethics' you will find for the noun: *moral principles that control or influence a person's behaviour*, and for the adjective, 'ethical': *morally correct or acceptable*. For the first time the dictionary definition is quite helpful! When applied to research, 'ethics' take on a particular meaning. This is obviously most acute in medical research and the biosciences, where ethical debates rage about the benefits and draw-backs of testing on animals, cloning (don't forget poor Dolly, the first example of animal cloning) and genetically modified food, etc.

The concern with ethical issues in social research, however, emerged after the deadly biomedical tests with human 'subjects' in Nazi Germany. For example, Nazi doctors experimented with prisoners of war to see how long people could survive in freezing water (Bulmer 2001: 49). An ethical question today is whether to use the results of this research which effectively murdered people, but may now be of use in saving others' lives? Should we destroy the results out of respect for those who suffered and their families and loved ones? Such experiments on humans led to the Nuremberg Code of 1949 which stated that individuals had to give *voluntary consent* to participate in any research (Holloway 1997: 55). This has had far-reaching implications for the way in which research is carried out today. Nowadays there are a number of professional organisations that set out explicit and comprehensive ethical codes and guidelines for researchers (for the website addresses, see Bryman 2001: 476). These can be a useful starting point for new researchers, for, as I have suggested, the topic of ethics is not clear-cut, as one person's ethical behaviour may not equate to another person's. Although you may not consider that ethics play much of a role in your research, you do need to reflect on a few things, especially if you intend working with qualitative methods, because, 'While all social research intrudes to some extent in people's lives, qualitative research often intrudes more. Some qualitative research deals with the most sensitive, intimate and innermost matters in people's lives, and ethical issues inevitably accom-pany the collection of such information' (Punch 2000b: 281). This is not to suggest that quantitative research is void of ethical considerations, as issues of confidentiality, honesty and accuracy arise in both types of research. Punch sums up the main areas in which ethical issues can arise in research as:

- harm
- consent
- deception
- privacy
- confidentiality.

You need to consider the likelihood of your research actually *harming* the people who participate in it. This may be difficult to assess, as the impact may be psychological, especially if you are asking people about a traumatic incident in their past. Physical harm to participants is unlikely to happen, although it is plausible as a consequence of the research or results, for example an IRA (Irish Republican Army) informer or mafia insider whose identity is found out.

Another key issue is that of the lack of informed consent. This issue was brought to the British public's attention recently by a news reporter who used covert tactics to infiltrate specific groups in society, most notoriously a gang of violent football hooligans (see box 44 below). The use of covert cameras and the lack of the participants' consent – however much we may dislike the people under investigation – is an ethical issue. However, in some cases it may be desirable actually to participate in direct observation *without* the group you are observing knowing who you are or what you are doing, which would, arguably, affect the way they behave in their 'natural setting'. The line between what is ethically acceptable and what is not is very difficult to establish. For example, Devine and Heath (1999: 189) argue that Rosenail, by publishing a book based on the experiences of other women at the Greenham camp (apart from herself), borders on flouting the principle of informed consent. How realistic is it to expect an author to track down former colleagues, friends, etc., to ask for their permission to publish anecdotes and stories that are made up of both the author's and their memories of past events?

Box 44   Ethics in research: Football hooliganism

I want you to reflect on the following case example and think through the reasons for your answers: a British journalist (Mr X) used a covert observation technique to uncover a number of unsavoury aspects of human life. Read the short narrative below and then shape your answers around the questions at the end.

Mr X went to great lengths in order to 'fit in' with a crowd of well-known hooligans, including allowing himself to be tattooed on the arm with a particular football club's name. The purpose of his investigative journalism was to uncover the origins of hooliganism and understand the inner workings of the leading perpetrators. Mr X wore a covert camera strapped to his waist, which allowed a fascinating insight into the workings of the hooligan group he joined. We witness people's motives for wanting repeatedly to cause (violent) disturbances (usually for the fun of it) and, more importantly, the reporter gains an insight into the structures, rules, norms and actions of the group.

Questions:

1 Is this method of investigation legitimate (bearing in mind the use of covert techniques and a lack of informed consent from participants)?
2 Regardless of what we think of the people observed (in this example, violent and dangerous), has the reporter gone against an accepted ethical code?
3 If this form of 'deception' is not legitimate, how can we find out about the structures, rules, norms and actions of such groups? Which other methods could bring similar results?
4 Note the pros and cons of this type of research.

The same goes for certain forms of deception in research. By 'deception' we mean the situation in which researchers deliberately give false information to respondents in order to elicit a particular response. The most famous case of this was the ethically dubious study carried out by Stanley Milgram in 1963, in which participants were deceived into believing that they were administering electric shocks to experimental subjects who answered questions wrongly (see Baron and Byrne 1997 for a summary of this case). Other studies use an (acceptable?) element of deception by, for example, dressing the researcher as a figure of authority to elicit and record a particular response from people. In this case it would obviously be counterproductive to explain to each and every person you meet what your research is about (see Bryman 2001: 484).

Respecting a person's privacy and confidentiality is also an ethical issue. If you interview someone and promise not to print her personal details, you must keep to that promise. First, because you would otherwise have deceived the person, which is in itself reprehensible, but secondly, you would tarnish the reputation of research in general. This is particularly important in the case of an interview with a person whom researchers after you may wish to meet. Once lied to, the subject is much less likely to give another researcher an interview.

Finally, the way in which you conduct your research, collect your data, analyse it and disseminate it all impact on ethical issues. You *must* avoid using sloppy research techniques, misinterpreting data, drawing conclusions from insufficient data and deliberately misrepresenting findings. The latter is enough to see you excluded from your studies and from consideration for any serious academic post for the rest of your working life.

▶ Continuum of ethics in research

The following continuum outlines the extreme positions taken on ethics in research, ranging from 'anything goes' at one end to 'universalism' at the other (I have taken these two categories from Bryman 2001: 478).

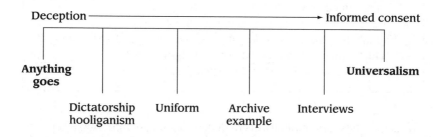

'Anything goes' is a position on ethics in research which argues for flexibility in the application of ethical standards, and 'universalism' takes the view that ethical precepts should never be broken. I have placed some examples along the continuum, starting at the left-hand side, which represents the greatest lack of informed consent and moving right towards maximum informed consent. As I go through the examples below, I want you to ask yourselves whether these examples are ethical or not and whether you would have placed them on the continuum as I have.

1   In the dictatorship and hooliganism example (see box 44 for details of the hooliganism case) I offer two different types of ethical conundrum: the first relates to researching dictatorships, which are, by their very nature, closed systems. Now, in my example, Fred wanted to produce a significant piece of work on a particular dictatorship on, let's say, state–society dynamics. Instead of simply using 'official' documents and statistics produced by the dictators, Fred has been given the opportunity of rummaging through 'secret' documents and files with the tacit consent of officials, who leave the room for a cigarette. Does Fred's rummaging, which, incidentally, leads to cutting-edge research, amount to ethically dubious research, because he did not have the consent of the authorities, albeit a dictatorship? The second example on this level is the use of the covert technique

to infiltrate hooligan groups described in box 44 above. The Milgram study (1963), mentioned earlier, would fall firmly under the 'deception' end of our continuum, as participants were given false information and subjected to psychological distress.

2 The second example pertains to researchers who act as a person of authority. For example, this could be someone dressed in a uniform escorting police officers on duty, taking part in arrests and pretending to be a policeman. Obviously this is deceiving those who are 'getting their collars felt', but the question remains, should we use uniforms to elicit specific responses from research subjects? Is this ethical?

3 A less straightforward example involves the use of archival sources. Lulu (not her real name) wanted to study the minutes of parliamentary groups in a particular political party archive. She wrote to the party seeking their permission, which, perhaps understandably for an organisation usually economical with the truth, said no. At the archive in question, the archivist just happened to leave Lulu alone in a room in which the parliamentary group minutes were kept and she could not help but take a peek. The archivist unfortunately died between data analysis and publication. In the preface of her book Lulu thanks the now-deceased archivist for giving his full permission to inspect the files on which part of Lulu's book is based. Is this unethical behaviour, given that the consequences of Lulu's actions and research for society could be argued to be positive (shedding light on corrupt politicians etc.)? Has anyone, apart from the party, been harmed?

4 The final example outlines an exemplary display of ethical behaviour *vis-à-vis* interview partners (informed consent). Vanessa interviewed some eighty women as part of a PhD on unemployment among women in East Germany. She informed the participants of the purpose of the research, cleared with them the sections of the (mostly recorded) interviews that she would publish and was discreet in regard to the interviewees' personal details. Being very open about the nature of your research can, however, increase the reluctance of people to participate in the first place, although, in Vanessa's case, people actually *wanted* to discuss their plight. A researcher who undertakes interviews needs to act ethically not only to maintain the integrity of the interviewer, which is of paramount importance, but also for the sake of research in general. Any unethical behaviour on a researcher's part may ruin future researchers' chances of interviewing the same or similar people.

I hope this short discussion has given you a taste of the difficulties surrounding ethics in research. As you can see, it is very difficult to arrive at a 'correct' answer – or ordering of the examples – to the ethical dilemmas posed in research. As Bulmer (2001: 49) points out:

> One general principle that runs through much of the discussion [on ethics and social research] is the need to strike a balance between society's desire, on the one hand, to expose the hidden processes at work in modern society and, on the other, to protect the privacy of the individuals and groups and to recognise that there are private spheres into which the social scientist may not, and perhaps even should not, penetrate.

Finally, the issue of covert research seems to excite researchers most. Advocates of this technique argue that the means (that is, the covert research) justifies the ends (that is, the research findings). Those opposed to or sceptical of this type of research rightly point out that no one is in a position to decide whether these means justify their (the researchers') ends. As Bulmer (2001: 56) rightly questions, 'whose causes are the right causes in social research?'

▶ Summary

The final chapter of this volume on the foundations of research has turned your attention to matters of plagiarism and ethics in research. The key points I wish you to take away from the above are as follows:

- Avoid accusations of plagiarism by learning the correct art of referencing at the beginning of your studies.
- Log and record *all* the information you draw upon as and when you gather it.
- Consider the ethical implications of your research strategy, whether it be quantitative, qualitative or a mixture of both.
- Stick to the principle of 'informed consent' as far as is practical and avoid unnecessary deception in research.

▶ Essential reading

Bryman, A. (2001) *Social Research Methods*, Oxford, Oxford University Press, chapter 24.

Bulmer, M. (2001) 'The Ethics of Social Research', in N. Gilbert (ed.), *Researching Social Life*, London, Thousand Oaks, CA and New Delhi, Sage, 2nd edition, chapter 4.

Rosamond, B. (2002) 'Plagiarism, Academic Norms and the Governance of the Profession', *Politics*, 22 (3), 167–74.

▶ Further reading

Denscombe, M. (2002) *Ground Rules for Good Research. A Ten-Point Guide for Social Researchers*, Buckingham, Open University Press, chapter 9.

Devine, F. and Heath, S. (1999) *Sociological Research Methods in Context*, Basingstoke, Palgrave Macmillan.

May, T. (2001) *Social Research. Issues, Methods and Process*, Buckingham, Open University Press, chapter 3.

9 Conclusion: Summary of Key Points

This book has been about the foundations of research, the things that underpin the research process and the language in which research is conducted. I have attempted to give some order to the often confused discourse surrounding research. Although I have been selective in my choice of tools and terms, I have sought to cover those which you will most certainly need and come across in your projects. In addition, I have sought to introduce you to some of the core debates or dichotomies in the human sciences, in particular, qualitative vs. quantitative research; structure vs. agency and inductive vs. deductive research. My intention has been to *familiarise* you with these debates rather than to offer an exhaustive account of each. It is my contention that by being *aware* of these debates and having knowledge of the core tools and terms used in the research process, you are best placed to begin your own projects. I have throughout adopted a somewhat humanist ideal in so far as I believe in getting to the root(s) of a problem or concept in order to understand it more fully. This is, however, not just a linguistic exercise: the importance of understanding what constitutes our research foundations places us in a good position from which to adjudicate contending perspectives on social phenomena. As I have suggested, criticising qualitative or quantitative work without understanding the principles upon which it is based and the process by which it has reached its conclusions, is poor scholarship. We must argue from a position of knowledge, if we are to contribute to constructive dialogue. The ten points below will, I hope, help you on the road to arguing from just such a position of knowledge. They are, in effect, a summary of the key points of the previous chapters:

1 First, familiarise yourself with the task ahead – be it a BA or MA dissertation or PhD – in particular, identify what is required for the degree you wish to undertake, how it is set out, what exactly is

required to pass. Look over previous successful undergraduate dissertations, MA dissertations and PhDs. Pay particular attention to how they are *structured* (for example, introduction, literature review, methodology section, case-study or empirical section, evaluation and conclusion).

2   Don't forget to familiarise yourself with, and remain consciously aware of, the *language* of research. By this I mean not only the individual concepts ('ideal type', 'paradigm', etc.), but also the -isms and -ologies of research. Like any language-learning exercise, you need to acquaint yourself with the core words, terms and phrases that are frequently used in research. Remember there will be a number of types of terms and phrases: for example, you will need to learn discipline-specific terms ('supply and demand' etc.), but there are also core research terms (methods, methodology, ontology, epistemology, etc.). If you learn the core terms correctly at the beginning of your project, the chances are that you will not fall into the trap of misusing and abusing them in your work. The result will be a more confident researcher, someone *not* shaken by the conference participant's question of 'but what's your ontological position then?' In turn, your work will be clearer, you will be able to engage with other scholars' work from a position of knowledge and understanding (i.e. you won't denigrate someone's work and their choice of methodology and methods just because they argue from a different research paradigm to you), and you are far more likely to produce a piece of clear and logical academic work. Additionally, you will understand research in a wider range of disciplines than just your own.

3   Also familiarise yourself with the technical language of beginning research. Even if you have no intention of using hypotheses or variables, you still need to be very clear what they mean and how they are used in various research strategies; otherwise you will not be in a position critically to appraise a piece of work which employs them. Remember, too, that you do not have to employ a hypothesis in your research, as a research question is often the best way to kick-start the literature-review process described in chapter 3. Research questions can be refined into hypotheses as you progress, if necessary.

4   This last point holds for many of the tools in research: choose these on the basis of the *most appropriate* for your work and *not* because you believe you must have a complex theory in order to produce good quality work. Good work is often ruined by an overelaboration of theoretical deliberation which fails to shed light on the empirical section of your project. Good theory ought to illuminate and make sense of the empirical reality you are presenting in your work. In

some projects a concept or concept-cluster will be more than adequate to do the job of giving order to your empirical enquiry, so don't feel forced into unnecessary complexity for the sake of it.

5 You should think of the following when learning the discourse of research. As a minimum, you need to familiarise yourself with the language of research in such diverse groups as: the tools used ('ideal type', 'concept', etc.); the different types of theory in research ('meta', 'grand', 'middle-range', etc.); the key terms ('ontology', 'epistemology', etc.); the most common research techniques ('interviews', 'regression analysis', 'discourse analysis', 'observation', etc.); the core research paradigms ('positivism', 'post-positivism' and 'interpretivism') and the major disciplinary perspectives within these (in particular, the ones in your discipline and the ones in cognate disciplines). If you learn these, you will be well equipped to read on and around your subject in the academic literature and fully participate in a research-methods course whilst being able fully to concentrate on the debates and arguments presented.

6 Reflect carefully on the level and unit of analysis you wish to concentrate on in your work. Take the time to sit down and actually think through your research proposal, research questions or hypotheses and sketch out how these lead you to particular levels and units of analysis and types of study. Take time to think about the structure–agency problem and how this impacts on your study. The emphasis here is on *reflection*, something most of us neglect as the pace of life dictates that we get things done quickly, then move on to the next task. You should actively incorporate time to *reflect* into your research plan. This should be distinguished from time spent relaxing, which is also a crucial part of the research process – we all need to regenerate – but what I mean is *active* reflection: forcing yourself to think through the constituent parts of your project and contemplating how they impact on one another.

7 Remember to remain aware of academic standards and begin proper referencing (and a bibliography) from the earliest opportunity. Avoid sloppy referencing and remain consistent; develop a solid method of note-taking and *always* record the bibliographical reference of the work you are reading and/or taking notes from.

8 You need to be aware that the research process rarely runs smoothly. All researchers, whether beginners or seasoned professionals, encounter new challenges and opportunities in every piece of research. Becoming disheartened is part and parcel of this process: not being able to get hold of specific documents; receiving no response from all those potential interview partners; having

difficulties in conceptualising the problem you are addressing; constantly discovering literature on and around your topic – all of these things are hard to plan for. The best advice is to expect the unexpected! In this way, you will not be too shocked and can adapt your project according to the problems and sometimes opportunities that can arise during research.

9   Remember there is more than one way to undertake research. There are a wide variety of disciplinary perspectives that seek to understand and often explain the subject they are focusing on. Such a plurality of approaches to studying social phenomena should be celebrated. However, a good piece of research in all disciplines, and research paradigms and the perspectives within them will exhibit a number of characteristics: researchers (and that means you) need to be very clear about the objectives of what they are trying to do; they need to reflect upon and make explicit the theoretical underpinnings of their research; they need to make clear how they will achieve the objectives they have set out; they need to show how their theoretical and conceptual approach sheds light on empirical reality (i.e. be clear about the *link* between theory and empirical data); they need to show how their work fits in with, complements or challenges existing work in that particular field.

10 Finally, try to avoid disciplinary entrenchment; keep an open mind about perspectives from outside your immediate discipline; remain true to yourself and your research projects/subjects by:

- avoiding corner-cutting in research (remember academic standards)
- remaining honest towards the people in your research (be it interviewees whom you've promised anonymity, or groups whom you have researched)
- avoiding the minimalist approach of 'scraping by' and throwing yourself into your research – being a researcher, studying a subject of your choice is a luxury you should enjoy. Good luck!

Appendix 1
Stages of the Research
Process

In this appendix I offer you a way of understanding the foundations of research by visualising their relationship to the research process in a boxes-and-arrows flow chart. The purpose here is to understand how the initial stages of research that have been introduced relate to one another and the end-destination of data collection and analysis. The second aim is to discuss how the research process can be broken up into stages. Although it may be argued that this is an artificial approach, given the *reflexive* nature of research, you will find that it is essential to have signposts to assist you during your studies. Signposts and stages are all intended to give order to a process that would otherwise be difficult to see as a whole. The model of the research process offered here is only *one* way (of many) of doing things; the important point is that everyone needs a road map of the research process, however artificial this may seem, or else they are very likely to go astray.

Figure 4 aims to give an overview of all the important research stages. It also shows the interconnectedness of the various steps. The arrows indicate the direction of progression from box 1 to box 12.

Spending time considering and planning out the first two stages of the research process, represented by boxes 1 and 2 in figure 4, is essential in order to carry out the subsequent stages to maximum effect. Boxes 1 and 2 represent what I described in chapters 1 and 2: that is, familiarising yourself with the nature of research, the mechanics of the process, and the tools needed to undertake it. Once you know what you are talking about, and no longer need to stop every five minutes to look up the meaning of specific research terms, you can get started on the various stages of the literature review on and around your topic (box 3).

As we have seen, this first encounter with the literature should confirm existing hunches or inform you (broadly) of the specific area and questions you wish to explore. By returning to the literature once the research questions or hypotheses have been refined and defined more

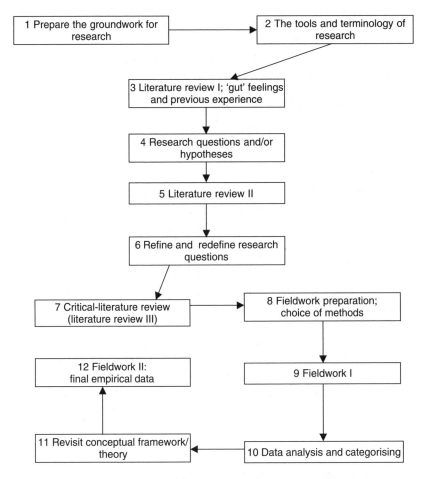

FIGURE 4 STEPS OF THE RESEARCH PROCESS

sharply (box 6), you can begin to structure and focus your further reading more clearly. This is essential, because the number and length of books, articles, texts and texts on texts can be simply overwhelming. You are now ready for the critical-literature review (box 7), after which your topic area, question(s) and methodological approach should be quite clear. You should also now be in a position to think about *how* you are going to answer the questions you have developed. This means deciding on the *type, unit* and *level* of analysis. The next stage is to choose which *method(s)* to employ and which *data* to collect for your study. Thus, very thorough preparations are needed for fieldwork (box 8), in which the necessary data to answer your research questions or validate and refute your hypotheses will be collected (box 9). Boxes 10 to 12 represent work that will be undertaken in the final stage of research, sometimes called the post-empirical stage. It is clear that original hypotheses and theoretical approaches need to be revisited whilst analysing and categorising the data, as these will, to a certain extent, have been guiding the choice of data in the first place. Box 12 represents the final possibility of adding to or filling any gaps in the project's empirical research. This is not as dramatic as it sounds, because by this stage it may only mean getting your hands on a specific document, speech or last-minute interview.

The purpose of figure 4 is to visualise the steps of the research process. By doing this, you can begin to see how they are all interwoven and bound by a certain *logic*. It is important to grasp 'the essentials and logic' of research (Punch 2000b: 7) before starting a large project: the diagram emphasises how the literature review(s), research questions, hypotheses and choice of methods used in a piece of research are inextricably linked. All of these components make up the research 'process', which should be seen as a 'series of linked activities moving from a beginning to an end' (Bouma and Atkinson 1995: 9). However, as we have seen, this does not mean, for example, that the literature review is completed early on and never returned to at subsequent stages of the process. Equally, all of these key research components are guided by our ontological and epistemological assumptions, discussed in detail in chapters 4 and 5 above.

▶ The stages of doctoral research

In this section I offer some ideas for visualising the key stages of research for doctoral students. Although the idea of stages of research may, as I have suggested, be somewhat artificial, in that they may not always follow the same sequence in every instance, there are certain elements of the research process that are common to all projects. Stages impose a kind of discipline on a complex business and many books on research offer models of various kinds. Table 10, however, is specifically designed to give an overview of the doctoral process. Reflecting this process, the table is divided into three broad stages, representing the three years of a doctoral degree, and subdivided into several smaller stages. The balance of work within the three broader

Table 10 POSSIBLE STAGES OF THE DOCTORAL PROCESS

	Sequence of Research Stages	Action
Stage I	1 Formulate your research problem; articulate your 'hunch' or tentative proposition	Learn tools and terminology of research; initial exploratory literature review
	2 Redefine and focus your topic and proposition	Second literature review. In addition, seek support by bouncing
	3 Select your variables or means of 'testing' your questions	ideas off peers/friends/supervisor and by attending conferences for networking; undertake critical-literature review
	4 Have clear central research questions or key hypotheses	Clarify your methodological approach
	5 Locate approach *vis-à-vis* others: begin writing the first chapter, setting out stages 1–4 above	Be familiar with debates/schools of thought/methods used and approaches on chosen topic; apply for external funding for fieldwork
	6 Select methods of enquiry	
	7 Produce a chapter outline of the whole thesis	
Stage II	8 Prepare ground for fieldwork	Locate data; contact archives, institutions, individuals, etc.
	9 Sketch out fieldwork plan	Give conference papers; possibly publish; seek external feedback on proposed topic
	10 Fieldwork	Data collection: interviews, archives, questionnaires, etc.
Stage III	11 Data analysis	Categorise data ready for analysis; analyse data
	12 Evaluate data	Possibly publish your preliminary results; analysis and
	13 Redefine central research questions or hypotheses in the light of empirical data analysis	interpretation of data; relate evidence to research question asked, draw conclusions
	14 Concentrate on writing-up stage	Revisit all previous stages; draw thesis together

stages will very much depend on your discipline and topic, but also your strengths and weaknesses as an individual and your financial position. The model is for a full-time student wishing to finish a doctorate in three years (this could represent the three full years *after* research training and taught components for some countries). A part-time student could simply label the three stages years 1–2, 3–4 and 5–6, respectively. The point of this figure is not to repeat the information given above, but rather to add a temporal dimension to the idea of research stages and to add an 'action' column, in which extra information on other activities that doctoral students could – and should – be doing is included.

The first and most important thing to note is that this model of the doctoral research process is an oversimplification of a complex undertaking (it is, after all, an abstraction based on my research, observation and personal experience). This book has not discussed the important theme of – and the table does not take into account – the psychological aspects of doing research, which can undoubtedly impinge on your ability to organise, structure and prioritise your work. Secondly, the stages of research are not divided and separate as in this artificial example; instead, a continuous process of *reflexivity* takes place throughout the whole period of study. You need constantly to refer back to your research questions or hypotheses, whilst analysing data or reviewing literature, to help you sort the wood from the trees – otherwise you could end up reading everything on a given topic – and so that you do not lose sight of what it is you are trying to research.

The 'action' column suggests activities that could, as far as possible, accompany and facilitate the logic of the research project. For example, none of the reflection and analysis mentioned above takes place in a vacuum with you hunched over a pile of books; rather there is a need for exposure and exchange of ideas not only with your supervisor but also with your peers and friends. Presenting your ideas to colleagues in seminars and at conferences is an essential part of academic life, along with gaining teaching experience as a postgraduate and publication, all of which will help you to refine and define your own ideas. One method of refining a research agenda is to tell a non-specialist (your mum, perhaps) in lay terms what it is exactly that you are studying or analysing. If you can sum up your topic and research questions crisply in a few sentences after having undertaken a thorough, and critical, review of the literature, you are ready to gather the evidence for your doctorate.

▶ Stage I

By the end of stage I (year 1) you should have underpinned your hunch or hypothesis with a detailed literature review and have already decided on an approach to adopt, including which methods and sources to use. In addition, you ought now to be in a position to apply to external funding bodies for fieldwork expenses (if applicable or available), a process that will take a long time to complete. For this reason, you must start thinking about it at the earliest opportunity. Equally, this is the time to go over everything you have done so far and put it into written form, for, although stage 14 suggests such a concept as a 'writing-up' stage, this is in fact a continual process and should certainly not be left to the very end. Like a runner who continually trains but refuses to race, you will never reach your goal if you put off the job of actually writing. And as a runner has to do a variety of different training sessions, from long-distance runs through to short, sharp, repetitions, in order to prepare for race-day, so your doctoral student's race-day also requires a variety of training regimes. Therefore, you need to write conference papers, notes and articles, and draft and redraft your thesis to prepare for the production of a very long text. The process of reflection includes constant feedback from supervisors, peers and friends on *written work* at every stage of the research process, thus preventing you from 'going off at a tangent', something to be wary of when planning long stints of fieldwork away from your institution.

▶ Stage II

This is around the time you should be thinking about upgrading to a PhD. This depends, of course, on your home institutional regulations, although many doctoral students are usually registered for an MPhil in the first instance, unless they already have an MA and have already undertaken substantial research training. This is also the time to think about presenting papers at conferences in order to receive external feedback from the wider academic community *before* embarking on fieldwork. The feedback process will assist you in compiling your fieldwork plan, or your 'map', which will remind you of your questions, *where* you need to go to find the data and *what* data to collect. The bulk of the data collection is ideally done in the second year, thus leaving the third year free for analysing and writing up the data. If you categorise your data clearly, if possible according to the chapters of your thesis, the task of analysing it and 'meshing' it with your (theoretical) approach will be much easier. After an initial analysis of empirical data, it may be possible to publish a paper using your literature review (indicating any 'gaps' found or a 'novel' interpretation of an old problem) and adding a little of the empirical data collected. It would not be wise to produce a huge paper on all of the major findings in the thesis, as this would make the book of the doctorate less attractive both to publishers and those likely to purchase it.

▶ Stage III

Stage III is dominated by the reflexivity mentioned earlier, for data collected needs to be analysed and interpreted with an eye to the central research questions or key hypotheses developed throughout the research and with an eye to *new* questions and avenues of enquiry that may open up. Again, it is a good idea to try to 'write up' during the period of analysis of data. Once the data analysis is finished, you should be able to enjoy editing the entire text. If you drop your thesis of, say, eight loose chapters on the floor, gather it up in a random order of chapter numbers, and find that it reads as well as before, something has gone radically wrong with its logic and structure. It is a good idea to have the thesis soft-bound at an early draft stage – and bear in mind this is only a draft – and read it from page 1 to the end to see if the constituent parts of your work actually join and flow together. It is interesting to witness how previously smooth-reading, self-contained chapters or sections suddenly crunch and grind against each other once bound and read together. Having the text soft-bound eases the task of smoothing out any abrupt changes in style or content and ensuring a common thread runs throughout the work. If you have been careful with referencing and bibliographical details, editing the whole thesis chapter by chapter can be a pleasurable experience. Your aim is to have one 'voice' running through the entire thesis, for your writing style will probably have changed as you progressed and learned how to sum up arguments succinctly (see Dunleavy 2003 for a more detailed discussion on style).

Appendix 2
Glossary of Research Terms

The following glossary of terms lists the words marked in bold throughout the main text. In some cases I have consulted etymological dictionaries in order to give the underlying meaning and origin of words, as going back to the roots of many terms is a good way of getting under the cloak of complexity. Most of the following words are either explained in the main text or their meanings are obvious from the context in which they have been used. The best idea is to look at both the glossary *and* the word or term in the text to get a better understanding of it. I have also included some aspects of the research process of interest to *particular* groups, for example, 'books on doctoral research'.

▶ Approach(es)

An approach describes the method used or steps taken in setting about a task or problem, especially with reference to which means of access or which sources are to be employed. Approaches are, like **methodologies**, particular ways of producing or getting at knowledge and as such are very much dependent on the view of the world taken by those that use them; to put it technically, they are informed by the paradigmatic assumptions upon which they are based. For example, a neoliberal approach to international relations would be underpinned by specific **ontological** and **epistemological** assumptions which would not necessarily be shared by other approaches to the same subject of enquiry in the same field. Confusion arises when academics use the term 'approaches' to mean specific disciplinary **perspectives**, specific theories and research **paradigms**.

▶ A priori

Simply, this term refers to knowledge based on theory rather than on experiment or experience. In general, it has come to be understood as a form of reasoning which is prior to experience and can be seen as the opposite of **empirical**. It is usually associated with a **deductive research** strategy.

▶ Case-study

Case-studies are a very popular way of structuring projects. A case-study is a restriction or narrowing of focus to one or more towns, individuals, organisations, etc., which are studied in great detail. Usually a variety of **quantitative** and **qualitative** research methods are used within case-study approaches, with the aim of shedding light on the object of study. Case-studies are an example of a specific *type* of approach. They represent particular strategies for research, involving empirical investigation of a particular contemporary phenomenon within its real-life context, and employing multiple sources of evidence.

▶ Causal/causality

Causation refers to the process of one event causing or producing another event (often referred to as 'cause and effect'). A causal relationship between two **variables** or things, for example, smoking and major diseases, is much clearer, and far less speculative, than a **correlation** between two variables or things. A great deal of **quantitative research**, and some **qualitative research**, attempts to identify causal relationships among the **variables** employed in the study.

▶ Concept(s)

The original meaning of the Latin term *conceptus* was 'a collecting, gathering or conceiving'. The modern-day equivalent encapsulates these sentiments. A concept is a general notion or an idea expressed in words or as a symbol. Concepts, like **theories**, range from the very simple to the complex, from the very specific to the highly abstract, and are regarded as the building blocks of theory (Blaikie 2000: 129). When concepts are **operationalised** in such a manner that they can be 'measured' to take on different numerical values, they are referred to as variables (Rudestam and Newton 1992: 19).

▶ Correlation

Correlation is the term used for any significant association (or covariation) between two or more **variables**. Importantly, correlation *does not mean nor imply* causation (Landman 2000: 224, emphasis added).

▶ Data

A mistake that almost all students and academics will make at one point in their studies concerns saving data on floppy disks and on the hard drive of their computers. As you will be writing something in the region of between fifty and three hundred pages and more for your **dissertations, theses** and notes, there is every reason to take great care when storing such information. First, make sure, if you are using computers at the university and one at home, that all computers have compatible word-processing programs. Use Rich Text Format (RTF) as far as possible, as this can be read and understood by most computer software. There is nothing more frustrating than saving work in one format only to find out once you arrive home or at work that your computer is unable to decipher the rows of hieroglyphics. Secondly, make sure you back up your work on disks, so that even if your computer(s) explodes or is stolen, you still have a faithful copy of your manuscript to hand. Make sure you keep the disks in a safe container. Also, set your computer, or have it set, to save your work every few minutes in case of a crash or power cut. Thirdly, record and log *all* your footnotes and bibliographical references *as you proceed*. If you manage to get into this habit, it will save you hours and nerves in the latter stages of your project. Finally, make sure you have an up-to-date virus detector on your computer(s), as a single virus could destroy hours of work in one click of the mouse.

▶ Data collection

Data collection is the process through which **empirical** data are produced and collected via a number of different data sources. There are many different methods of data collection, associated with both **quantitative** and **qualitative research**, and a wide range of sources of data that can be collected.

▶ Deductive research

Deductive research is that which begins with clear assumptions or previous knowledge in order to understand a particular problem or find the answer to a problem. Above all, it is a label given to theory-driven research as opposed to research that seeks to derive **theories** from **empirical** evidence (see **inductive research**). The term 'hypothetico-deductive' is reserved for such research that relates to or makes use of the method of proposing **hypotheses** and testing their acceptability or falsity by checking their logical consequences are consistent with **empirical** data. It is doubtful whether in real-life research the so-called 'inductive–deductive' dichotomy (see chapter 6 for more on this) is anywhere near as clear-cut as it is made out to be.

▶ Dependent variable

The dependent variable is the thing which is caused or affected by the **independent variable**. In the example in the text of chapter 3, the dependent variable was worsening public attitudes towards Germany, which were fuelled by the **independent variable** of print-media representation of Germany in the USA. The dependent variable is also known as the outcome variable or endogenous variable (Landman 2000: 224–5). It is important to remember that every dependent variable can also be an **independent variable**; it is the researcher who chooses.

▶ Dissertation

In the UK it is usual to use the term 'dissertation' for a relatively long piece of work over and above the length of an extended essay. Students studying for a first degree or MA usually complete a dissertation as opposed to a **thesis** (see below). To add to the confusion, the term 'dissertation' is used in other countries, such as the US and Germany, to refer to a doctoral **thesis**.

▶ Doctoral research (further reading)

Books abound on the topic of undertaking research, dealing with a variety of factors relevant to the entirety of a research project. The majority of textbooks on the market deal with the process of research in general. There are a number of good texts that aim to cover a wide range of research situations and levels, relevant to doctoral students as much as to seasoned academics, policy makers and practitioners (for example, Bell 1993; Blaxter et al. 1997; Blaikie 2000; Robson 1995, 2002). Although these books are not explicitly aimed at Master's or doctoral students, it is to them and their ilk that most postgraduates turn.

A recent attempt to focus a particular text on this area was undertaken by Peter Burnham in his edited volume, *Surviving the Research Process in Politics* (1997). The result is a multi-authored book consisting of a number of important topics relating to doctoral research. Some chapters have direct relevance to parts of the doctoral process (in politics), while others are more concerned with factors that can influence it, for example working full-time whilst studying. The book is not designed to explain the building blocks of research or to touch on the inherent logic of the process, but Burnham's useful introductory chapter, and his chapter on the **viva**, along with a few chapters on methods used in research, do shed light on some important components of a PhD.

Working for a Doctorate (Graves and Varma 1999) is another useful multi-authored book, with topics ranging from 'Intercultural Issues' and 'Gender Issues' to 'Financing a Doctorate'. Denis Lawton offers an excellent overview of how to succeed in postgraduate studies and Derek May tackles the central issue of time management.

Perhaps the best known and most widely sold book on PhD research is *How to Get a PhD* (Phillips and Pugh 1994). This text addresses both the supervisor and the supervisee by offering advice on many aspects of the doctoral process. This necessarily covers a lot of ground, as the book does not narrow its focus to any specific area (e.g. social sciences), resulting in a broad approach to the PhD project. The Phillips and Pugh book has some very important chapters, such as those on psychological aspects of the PhD research and the student–supervisor relationship. Try also Wisker (2001) for some handy hints on the PhD process and Dunleavy (2003) for a guide on how to write a doctorate, how to finish it and how to get your work published.

▶ Empirical

From the Latin *empiricus*, meaning 'experience', empirical has come to mean the opposite of theoretical: that is, that which is derived from, guided by or based on observation, experiments or experience rather than ideas or **theories** (see also **a priori**). Many philosophical research positions and academic **perspectives** have been built up around empiricism, the core belief of which is that all knowledge is derived from sense-experience as opposed to learning through rational thinking. The term is generally used in combinations such as empirical evidence, empirical data, empirical (as opposed to theoretical) study or research and empirical knowledge.

▶ Epistemology, epistemological

Derived from the Greek words *episteme* (knowledge) and *logos* (reason), epistemology is the **theory** of knowledge. Epistemological considerations depend on beliefs about the nature of knowledge. Also, assumptions about forms of knowledge, access to knowledge and ways of acquiring and gathering knowledge are epistemological issues (Holloway 1997: 54). All of the above impact on the research process and, importantly, **data collection** and analysis. Epistemology refers to the 'strategies through which a particular theory gathers knowledge and ensures that its reading of phenomena is superior to rival theories' (Rosamond 2000: 7, 199) (see chapter 4 for examples of how your epistemological position interlinks with other components of the research process).

▶ Ethnographic research

From the noun 'ethnography', the original meaning of which was 'the description of races', ethnographical research is characterised by long stays in the field in which the researcher submerges himself or herself in the culture, language and day-to-day lives of those she is studying. The aim is to find patterns of power between specific group-members, study symbols of identity formation, the use of language, and so on.

▶ Evaluation

The evaluation of data is one of the last stages of research, in which the researcher determines the significance, value and utility of her findings by careful and systematic analysis. At this stage, data are usually coded or categorised to assist the process.

▶ Fieldwork

The activity of **data collection**: a term related to the **empirical** side of research in which data are gathered on site or on location. It usually involves spending a sustained amount of time at the area under study, or in archives, or interviewing. During fieldwork, data are gathered with which to observe relationships between certain selected **variables**, or new relationships and variables may be found.

▶ Grounded theory

Grounded theory, a phrase coined by B. G. Glaser and A. L. Strauss in the 1960s, refers to a research strategy that does not start with a **hypothesis**, but rather seeks relationships between concepts once the data have been collected. This type of research involves the interpretation of data in their social and cultural contexts (see Holloway 1997: 80–7 and chapter 6 for a further explanation).

▶ Hermeneutics

Hermeneutics pertains to interpretation and can be understood as a form of data analysis which seeks to analyse a text from the perspective of the person who penned it, whilst emphasising the social and historical context within which it was produced.

▶ Heuristic tool

Heuristic is an adjective that basically means 'involving or serving as an aid to discovering or learning', in particular by trial-and-error methods. Heuristic research tools are conceptual devices that help the researcher to obtain specific information. One example of this is Weber's **ideal type** (see chapter 2 for an example of an ideal type).

▶ Hypothesis, hypotheses

A hypothesis is a proposition, set of propositions or assumption put forward for **empirical** testing; a testable proposition about the relationship between two or more events or **concepts**. Hypotheses are traditionally linked to the **deductive** method of research, whereby such propositions are derived from theory to provide the 'why' questions in social research (Blaikie 2000: 163). A hypothesis consists of an **independent** and **dependent variable** and contains a **causal** proposition (see chapter 3 for an example of how formally to set out hypotheses).

▶ **Ideal type**

An ideal type is a construct – a description of a phenomenon in its abstract form which can assist in comparing and classifying specific phenomena (Holloway 1997: 90). According to the person attributed with inventing it, an ideal type is:

> not a description of reality but it aims to give unambiguous means of expression to such a description.... An ideal type is formed by the one-sided *accentuation* of one or more points of view and by the synthesis of a great many diffuse, discrete, more or less present and occasionally absent *concrete individual* phenomena, which are arranged according to those one-sidedly emphasized viewpoints into a unified *analytical* construct. In its conceptual purity, this mental construct cannot be found empirically anywhere in reality. (Weber 1949: 90)

▶ **Independent variable**

See **dependent variable**. Shown as 'X' in formal models, the independent variable is also known as a **causal** variable, an explanatory variable or an exogenous variable (Landman 2000: 226).

▶ **Inductive research**

Induction is, broadly, a mode of reasoning from the particular to the general, and inductive research can be understood as research which draws conclusions from specific **empirical** data (the particular) and attempts to generalise from them (the general), leading to more abstract ideas, including **theories** (see chapter 6).

▶ Inference

Both **quantitative** and **qualitative research** use inference. The act of inferring involves passing from one proposition or statement considered true, to another whose truth is believed to follow from that of the former. Inference can be by deductive or inductive methods and is particularly used in connection with statistical calculations, with which the researcher attempts to extrapolate from sample data to generalisations (see Encyclopaedia Britannica on-line).

▶ Literature review

This may be known as a review of the literature or literature survey. Usually one of the first steps in the research process is a review of the literature on and around the subject of enquiry. Its main functions are to avoid duplication, 'discover' gaps in research (or areas to which you can add knowledge) and 'place' your own approach among the work and approaches of other scholars. In this book I have highlighted three types of literature review: the initial 'dip' stage; the second review in which research questions and/or **hypotheses** are developed and defined and the final 'critical-literature review' (see chapter 3).

▶ Macro

Macro means 'long' or 'large' in Greek and, in social research, pertains to a level of analysis which focuses on countries, systems, structures, institutions and organisations, as opposed to individual actors.

▶ Methodology, methodologies

Methodology is a branch of science concerned with methods and techniques of scientific enquiry; in particular, with investigating the potential and limitations of particular techniques or procedures. The term pertains to the science and study of methods and the assumptions about the ways in which knowledge is produced. A certain methodological approach will be underpinned by and reflect specific **ontological** and **epistemological** assumptions. These assumptions will determine the *choice* of approach and methods adopted in a given study by emphasising particular ways of knowing and finding out about the world. Methodology deals with the logic of enquiry, of how **theories** can be generated and subsequently tested. Methodology is *very* often confused and used interchangeably with **methods**.

▶ Methods

The original Greek meaning of method was 'the pursuit of knowledge'. In a sense, this is still what it means in research today, in as much as the methods a researcher employs in a study, that is, the techniques and procedures used to collect and analyse data, are the tools with which we pursue knowledge. There is a wide variety of methods, ranging from discourse analysis, archival retrieval of data, interviews, direct observation, comparisons of data, and documentary analysis to surveys, questionnaires and statistics. Certain methods can be used in either **qualitative** or **quantitative research**. Although there is a general and artificial division between the two types of approach, the best social-science research is often carried out using a combination of both. The methods employed in a project are usually informed by the methodology chosen and the questions asked, rather than the other way around.

▶ Micro

The original Greek meaning is 'small' and, in social research, 'micro' tends to refer to a level of analysis that includes the study of individuals as opposed to institutions and organisations.

▶ Model

Models are replications of reality. Toy cars are models of the real thing on a smaller scale; in social science, researchers try to construct a simplification of reality by setting out models that indicate links between specific components. Usually, arrows and boxes are used to depict and attempt to make explicit significant relationships between specific aspects of the model; thus a model 'enables the formulation of empirically testable propositions regarding the nature of these relationships' (Frankfort-Nachmias and Nachmias 1992: 44).

▶ Ontology/ontological

Ontology is a branch of metaphysics concerned with the nature of being. The first part of the word comes from the Greek verb equivalent to the English 'to be'. It can be understood as the basic image of social reality upon which a **theory** is based. It can, however, be better understood as the way in which we view the world; it is our starting point in research, upon which the rest of the process is based. Ontological claims are 'claims and assumptions that are made about the nature of social reality, claims about what exists, what it looks like, what units make it up and how these units interact with each other. In short, ontological assumptions are concerned with what we believe constitutes social reality. (Blaikie 2000: 8). Your 'ontological position', whether you know it or not, is implicit even before you choose your topic of study. We all have views on how the world is made up and what the most important components of the social world are.

▶ Operationalise, operationalising

To operationalise a concept is simply to turn it into a **variable** which can be 'measured' in fieldwork or in the gathering of information. The first stage is to develop or find a suitable concept that can be turned into a variable. Then we need to translate these abstract notions into something which can record or 'measure' data. In studies of democracies, for example, the concept of political engagement could be used to gauge the civic vibrancy of a region. We would need to find a suitable variable for this concept, for example voting levels or membership figures of political parties or associations. We would thus have 'operationalised' the concept of political engagement in research.

▶ Paradigm(s)

Originally meaning 'pattern' or 'model', paradigm has come to mean three different things. First, it is 'an established academic approach' in a specific discipline in which academics use a common terminology, common **theories** based on agreed paradigmatic assumptions and agreed **methods** and practices (see Rosamond 2000: 192). Paradigms, which act as organising frameworks for researchers, are often overtaken or replaced by others, leading to what is commonly called a 'paradigm shift': that is, the former majority approach is superseded by a new approach, using different terminology, **theories, methods** and practices. Secondly, the term can be used to sum up broad-brush approaches to social phenomena – for example, 'top-down' or 'bottom-up' paradigms of research. Thirdly, paradigm is employed to distinguish between research traditions. The key research paradigms, positivism, post-positivism (critical realism) and interpretivism, are outlined in chapter 5.

▶ Parsimony

A parsimonious explanation is considered to be one which 'uses the least amount of evidence to explain the most amount of variation' (Landman 2000: 227).

▶ Perspective(s)

An academic perspective pertains to (a) certain approaches *within* a discipline, for example, new institutionalism and rational choice in political science, and (b) approaches that transcend narrow academic disciplines, for example a feminist or post-modern perspective.

▶ Professional associations

At the beginning of your studies, you should consider joining an association relevant to your thesis topic, for example the PSA (Political Studies Association, www.psa.ac.uk) or the BSA (British Sociological Association, www.britsoc.org.uk) in the UK or the APSA (American Political Science Association, www.apsanet.org) in the USA, or your disciplinary equivalent. Each discipline will have a specific association through which you gain access to a number of useful things. For example, on joining, usually at a subsidised rate, you can go to annual conferences, workshops and specialist subgroups that may be more relevant to your topic. Some associations even send out newsletters and journals, both of which are important while you are studying: the newsletter contains information on forthcoming events, and the journal is essential reading for postgraduate students working at the 'cutting edge' of research. Look out for e-mail circulation lists that are usually free to join and provide instant updates on conferences, new publications, and so on. Many associations also offer guidance on how to undertake research in specific disciplines. These types of gatherings offer an ideal opportunity for 'networking' among like-minded people, both students and staff; something to bear in mind if you intend staying in academia. In addition, there is something quite reassuring in seeing the face behind the name of an author of a book you have read. You can see that these authors are human after all! Some associations have graduate networks through which you can make contact with people who are working in a similar field or who are experiencing similar problems.

▶ Qualitative (research)

Qualitative is derived from 'quality', a term coined by Plato to mean 'of what kind'. Qualitative research is characterised by the use of methods that attempt to examine 'inherent traits, characteristics, and qualities of the political objects of inquiry' (Landman 2000: 227). The **methods** used in this type of research tend to be more interpretative in nature.

▶ Quantitative (research)

This term is derived from 'quantity', and pertains to numbers. Quantitative research employs methods with the intention of being able to produce data that can be quantified (counted, measured, weighed, enumerated, and so manipulated and compared mathematically). This type of research is interested in finding general patterns and relationships among **variables**, including for some testing **theories** and making predictions (Ragin 1994: 132–6).

▶ Research questions

Research questions are intended to guide your enquiries. By establishing general research questions, the researcher begins to narrow his or her focus of enquiry, something that is essential given the amount of information available. A general research question would need to be answerable: for example, 'Does the fact that students have to take term-time jobs to subsist impact on their examination performance?' The next stage is to develop more specific research questions and, if appropriate, **hypotheses**. The former would sharpen the study's focus even more, while the latter would give you a (**causal**) statement to guide your studies: for example, 'Full-time students of economics who take term-time jobs perform worse than those economics students who do not', i.e. working in term-time jobs *is the cause* of the poor results.

▶ Research strategy

A research strategy is the manner in which you approach your research topic, for example, inductively or deductively. This choice will impact on how you formulate your **research questions** or **hypotheses**, the level and units of analysis you choose and the type of study and the sources of data to be collected.

▶ Sources

Sources are crucial to the research process. They represent the evidence with which to test **theories**, propositions, hunches, and so on. Without **empirical** evidence in the form of, for example, documents, statistics, interview transcripts, etc., **hypotheses** in the human sciences would remain untested, an unsatisfactory state of affairs unless the purpose of research was to contribute to theoretical debates. There is no general transdisciplinary consensus on the usefulness of some sources as opposed to others, as is the case with **methods, methodologies, perspectives** and **theories**. However, the theoretical underpinnings of your project will have a great impact on which sources you will use, given that your research questions will point you to the sources to gather and that the questions you ask are guided by your ontological and epistemological positions. Generally, a wide source base will lessen the chance of an invalid study.

▶ Structure and agency problem

Stuart McAnulla nicely sums up the problem of structure and agency as follows:

> Fundamentally, the debate concerns the issue of to what extent we as actors have the ability to shape our destiny as against the extent to

which our lives are structured in ways out of our control; the degree to which our fate is determined by external forces. Agency refers to individual or group abilities (intentional or otherwise) to affect their environment. Structure usually refers to context: the material conditions which define the range of actions available to actors. (2002: 271)

▶ Theory, theories

There are many different types of theory, ranging from metatheory through grand and middle-range to **grounded theory** (the difference between theories is their degree of abstraction and their scope). Metatheory pertains to the underpinnings of your research: your onto-logical and epistemological positions. Grand theory is very abstract and presents a conceptual scheme 'intended to represent the important features of a total society' (Blaikie 2000: 144). Middle-range theories, probably the most commonly used in research, are limited to a specific domain, for example the labour process (Bryman 2001: 6). (For a defin-ition of **grounded theory**, see the entry in the glossary.) A theory is a guess about the way things are. Theories are abstract notions which assert specific relationships between **concepts**. In research, theories are linked to *explanation* as opposed to *description*. The abstract ideas and propositions contained in theory are generally tested in **fieldwork** by the **collection of data**. A good theory will be generalisable and able to be employed in different contexts to the original. In the words of Karl Popper, theories are 'nets cast to catch what we call "the world": to rationalise, to explain and to master it. We endeavour to make the mesh ever finer and finer' (Popper 2000: 59).

All research is theoretical, whether it wants to be or not, because a person who suggests she is 'simply getting on with the job of research by starting with some empirical data or documents' has, without knowing it, made a number of claims about the nature of knowledge, the methods she is using and the sources the methods produce.

▶ Thesis

A thesis is the large body of written work necessary for gaining a PhD or MPhil. The former usually requires a work of between 80,000 and 120,000 words, whereas the latter usually requires between 20,000 and 60,000 words.

▶ Thick description

This is a detailed account of field experiences which contextualises and makes explicit the patterns of cultural and social relationships drawn from observations in the field. Thick description builds up a clear picture of the individuals and groups in the context of their culture and the setting in which they live (see Holloway 1997: 154).

▶ Triangulation, triangulated

The term has come to be associated with the practice of drawing on a variety of data sources, which are cross-checked with one another to limit the chances of bias in the methods or sources employed. It is common practice to attempt to measure one particular **variable** using a variety of different methods, for example mixing statistical analysis with **qualitative** methods to gain further insights into 'reality' on the ground. There is a difference between triangulating methods and the triangulation of data resulting from diverse sources.

▶ Typology

The early Greek philosophers, Socrates, Plato and Aristotle, all used some form of categorisation. Today, a typology, like a taxonomy, can be seen as a classificatory system which the researcher uses to categorise data. These devices can be seen as loose frameworks within which to organise and systematise our observations. Like **ideal types**, typologies and taxonomies do not provide us with explanation; rather they describe empirical phenomena by fitting them into a set of categories. However, typologies, especially in comparative analyses, can be looked upon as the first stage of theory building, as researchers attempt to test the influence of one or more variables on other variables.

▶ Validating

This is very similar in meaning to 'verifying'; see **verifiability of data**. In research, scholars attempt to achieve 'internal validity' and 'external validity' of their research. The former refers to the extent to which researchers can demonstrate that they have evidence for the statements and descriptions they make; the latter refers to a study's generalisability: that is, the relevance of the study's statements over and above the case-study used (see Holloway 1997: 159–62).

▶ Value-free

This phrase pertains to the notion of value neutrality among researchers when investigating the social world. This ideal has come to be seen as impossible in social science research, as all investigators have particular perspectives. However, as a scholar one should make the following *absolutely clear*: the choices of **theoretical** approaches; the **variables** used in the study and the research design, and any limitations of the inferences from the work (see Landman 2000: 51).

▶ Variables

Variables are concepts which vary in amount or kind. Researchers **operationalise concepts** by translating them into variables that can be 'measured' and used in gathering information.

▶ Verifiability of data

The verb to verify means literally 'to prove to be true' or 'test the correctness, accuracy or reality of'. In research, one speaks of the verifiability of findings or data: that is, the ability to check the data a researcher has gathered by following the same methods or **data collection** and data-analysis techniques.

▶ Viva (voce)

The viva voce, literally the 'living voice', is an oral examination. For PhD students, and some MPhil students, it marks the culmination of their efforts and is a process carried out behind closed doors – in the majority of institutions – between the candidate, the internal and external examiners, and perhaps a chairperson. If successful, the viva can be understood as a passage from a student to a professional 'Dr'. The title, however, is officially only allowed to be used after graduation.

The purpose of a viva is to confirm that the candidate is the author of the work submitted and has an appropriate grasp of the knowledge on and around her field of study.

▶ Working hypothesis

A working hypothesis is a proposition which helps guide subsequent research and which can be defined and refined in the light of further research.

Bibliography

Abercrombie, N., Hill, S. and Turner, B. S. (eds) (1984) *The Penguin Dictionary of Sociology*, Harmondsworth, Penguin.

Archer, M. (1995) *Realist Social Theory: The Morphogenetic Approach*, Cambridge, Cambridge University Press.

Archer, M., Bhaskar, R., Collier, A., Lawson, T. and Norrie, A. (eds) (1998) *Critical Realism. Essential Readings*, London and New York, Routledge.

Aristotle (1948) *Politics*, Oxford, Clarendon Press (ed. E. Baker).

Baron, R. A. and Byrne, D. (1997) *Social Psychology*, Boston, MA, Allyn & Bacon.

Bell, J. (1993) *Doing Your Research Project. A Guide to First-Time Researchers in Education and Social Science*, Buckingham, Open University Press.

Blaikie, N. (2000) *Designing Social Research*, Cambridge, Polity Press.

Blaxter, L., Hughes, C. and Tight, M. (1997) *How to Research*, Buckingham, Open University Press.

Boland, L. A. (2001) 'Neo-Classical Economics', in A. Kuper and J. Kuper (eds), *The Social Science Encyclopedia*, pp. 567–9.

Bouma, G. D. and Atkinson, G. B. J. (1995) *A Handbook of Social Research. A Comprehensive and Practical Guide for Students*, New York, Oxford University Press.

Bryman, A. (1995) *Research Methods and Organization Studies*, London and New York, Routledge.

Bryman, A. (2001) *Social Research Methods*, Oxford, Oxford University Press.

Bryman, A. and Cramer, D. (1994) *Analysis for Social Scientists*, London, Routledge, revised edn.

Bulmer, M. (2001) 'The Ethics of Social Research', in N. Gilbert (ed.), *Researching Social Life*, London, Thousand Oaks, CA and New Delhi, Sage, 2nd edn.

Bulmer, S. and Paterson, W. (1989). West Germany's role in Europe: 'Man-Mountain' or 'Semi-Gulliver'? *Journal of Common Market Studies*, 28(2), 95–117.

Burnham, P. (ed.) (1997) *Surviving the Research Process in Politics*, London and Washington, DC, Pinter.

Calhoun, C., Gerteis, J., Moody, J., Pfaff, S., Schmidt, K. and Virk, I. (eds) (2002a) *Classical Sociological Theory*, Oxford, Blackwell.

Calhoun, C., Gerteis, J., Moody, J., Pfaff, S. and Virk, I. (eds) (2002b) *Contemporary Sociological Theory*, Oxford, Blackwell.

Cannell, F. and Green, S. (2001) 'Patriarchy', in A. Kuper and J. Kuper (eds), 592.

Clough, P. and Nutbrown, C. (2002) *A Student's Guide to Methodology*, London, Thousand Oaks, CA and New Delhi, Sage.

Coleman, J. (1988) 'Social Capital in the Creation of Human Capital', *American Journal of Sociology*, 94, 13–39, reprinted in I. Dasgupta and P. Serageldin (eds) (2000), *Social Capital. A Multifaceted Perspective*, Washington, DC, World Bank.

Crotty, M. (1998) *The Foundations of Social Research. Meaning and Perspective in the Research Process*, London, Thousand Oaks, CA and New Delhi, Sage.

Culpepper, P. D. (2003). *Creating Cooperation: How States Develop Human Capital in Europe*, Ithaca, NY and London, Cornell University Press.

Danermark, B., Ekström, M., Jakobsen, L. and Karlsson, J. (2002) *Explaining Society. Critical Realism in the Social Sciences*, London and New York, Routledge.

de Tocqueville, A. (1969) *Democracy in America*, ed. J. P. Mayer, trans. George Lawrence, Garden City, NY, Anchor Books.

Delanty, G. (2000) *Social Science. Beyond Constructivism and Realism*, Buckingham, Open University Press.

Denscombe, M. (2002) *Ground Rules for Good Research. A Ten-Point Guide for Social Researchers*, Buckingham, Open University Press.

Devine, F. and Heath, S. (1999) *Sociological Research Methods in Context*, Basingstoke, Palgrave Macmillan.

Dogan, M. (2000) 'Political Science and the Other Social Sciences', in R. E. Goodin and H.-D., Klingemann, *A New Handbook of Political Science*, Oxford, Oxford University Press.

Dunleavy, P. (2003) *Authoring a PhD: How to Plan, Draft, Write and Finish a Doctoral Thesis or Dissertation*, Basingstoke, Palgrave Macmillan.

Engerman, S. L. (2000) 'Max Weber as Economist and Economic Historian', in S. Turner (ed.), *The Cambridge Companion to Weber*, Cambridge, Cambridge University Press.

Fairbairn, G. J. and Winch, C. (2000) *Reading, Writing and Reasoning. A Guide for Students*, Buckingham and Philadelphia, PA, Open University Press, 2nd edn.

Flyvbjerg, B. (2001) *Making Social Science Matter. Why Social Inquiry Fails and How it Can Succeed Again*, Cambridge, Cambridge University Press.

Frankfort-Nachmias, C. and Nachmias, D. (1992) *Research Methods in the Social Sciences*, London, Edward Arnold, 4th edn.

Friedman, M. (1953) *Essays in Positive Economics*, Chicago and London, University of Chicago Press.

Friedrich, C. and Brzezinski, Z. (1956/75) *Totalitarian Dictatorship and Autocracy*, Cambridge, MA, Harvard University Press.

Fulbrook, M. (2002) *Historical Theory*, London and New York, Routledge.

Geertz, C. (1973) *The Interpretation of Cultures*, New York, Basic Books.

Gerring, J. (2001) *Social Science Methodology. A Criterial Framework*, Cambridge, Cambridge University Press.

Giddens, A. (1979) 'Theory of Structuration', in Calhoun et al. (2002b), 232–43.

Giddens, A. (2001) *Sociology*, Cambridge, Polity, 4th edn.

Gilbert, N (ed.) (2001) *Researching Social Life*, London, Thousand Oaks, CA and New Delhi, Sage.

Grant, W. (2000) 'Elite Interviewing: A Practical Guide', Institute for German Studies, Birmingham University, Discussion Paper No. 11.

Graves, N. and Varma, V. (eds) (1999) *Working for a Doctorate. A Guide for the Humanities and Social Sciences*, London/New York, Routledge.

Grayling, A. C. (2002) *The Reason of Things. Living with Philosophy*, London, Weidenfeld & Nicolson.

Grix, J. (2000) *The Role of the Masses in the Collapse of the GDR*, Basingstoke, Palgrave Macmillan.

Grix, J. (2001a) *Demystifying Postgraduate Research. From MA to PhD*, Birmingham, University of Birmingham Press.

Grix, J. (2001b) 'Social Capital as a Concept in the Social Sciences: The Current State of the Debate', *Democratization*, 8(3), 189–210.

Grix, J. (ed.) (2002a) *Approaches to the Study of Contemporary Germany: Research Methodologies in German Studies*, Birmingham, University of Birmingham Press, pp. 1–21.

Grix, J. (2002b) 'Introducing Students to the Generic Terminology of Social Research', *Politics*, 22(3), 175–85.

Grix, J. and Knowles, V. (2003) 'The Euroregion – A Social Capital Maximiser? The Case of the German-Polish Euroregion Pro Europa Viadrina', *Regional and Federal Studies*, special edn, 12(4), 156–79.

Guba, E. G. and Lincoln, Y. S. (1998) 'Competing Paradigms in Qualitative Research', in N. K. Denzin and Y. S. Lincoln (eds), *The Landscape of Qualitative Research. Theories and Issues*, London Thousand Oaks, CA and New Delhi, Sage.

Hall, P. (1999) 'Social Capital in Britain', *British Journal of Political Science*, 29(3) (July), 417–61.

Hart, C. (2000) *Doing a Literature Review*, London, Sage.

Hay, C. (1995) 'Structure and Agency', in D. Marsh and G. Stoker (eds), *Theory and Methods in Political Science*, Basingstoke, Palgrave Macmillan.

Hay, C. (2002) *Political Analysis*, Basingstoke, Palgrave Macmillan.

Heywood, A. (2002) *Politics*, Basingstoke, Palgrave Macmillan.

Hirschman, A. O. (1970) *Exit, Voice and Loyalty. Responses to Decline in Firms, Organizations and States*, Cambridge, MA and London, Harvard University Press.

Hoffman, A. and Knowles, V. (1999) 'Germany and the Reshaping of Europe. Identifying Interests – The Role of Discourse Analysis', ESRC-IGS Working Paper No. 9.

Hoggart, K., Lees, L. and Davies, A. (eds) (2002) *Researching Human Geography*, London, Arnold.

Hollis, M. (1999) *The Philosophy of Social Science*, Cambridge, Cambridge University Press.

Hollis, M. and Smith, S. (1990) *Explaining and Understanding International Relations*, Oxford, Oxford University Press.

Holloway, I. (1997) *Basic Concepts for Qualitative Research*, Oxford, Blackwell Science.

Hughes, J. and Sharrock, W. (1997) *The Philosophy of Social Research*, London and New York, Longman, 3rd edn.

Hutton, W. (1996) *The State We're In*, London, Vintage.

Hutton, W. (1999) *The Stakeholding Society, Writings on Politics and Economics*, Cambridge, Polity Press.

Jenkins, R. (2002) *Foundations of Sociology. Towards a Better Understanding of the Human World*, Basingstoke, Palgrave Macmillan.

Johnston, R. T., Gregory, D., Pratt, G. and Watts, M. (eds) (2000) *The Dictionary of Human Geography*, Blackwell, Oxford, 4th edn.

Jones, D. (2002) 'Contemporary Theorising', in I. Marsh (ed.), *Theory and Practice in Sociology*, Harlow, Prentice Hall, pp. 220–56.

Kerr, P. (2003) 'Keeping it real! Evolution in Political Science: A Reply to Kay and Curry', *British Journal of Politics and International Relations*, 5 (1), February, 118–28.

King, G., Keohane, O. and Verba, S. (1994) *Designing Social Inquiry. Scientific Inference in Qualitative Research*, Princeton, NJ, Princeton University Press.

Klein, E. (1966 and 1967) *A Comprehensive Etymological Dictionary of the English Language*, Amsterdam, London and New York, Elsevier, vols I–III.

Kuhn, T. S. (1996) *The Structure of Scientific Revolutions*, Chicago and London, University of Chicago Press.

Kumar, R. (1999) *Research Methodology. A Step-By-Step Guide for Beginners*, London, Thousand Oaks, CA and New Delhi, Sage.

Kuper, A. and Kuper, J. (eds) (2001) *The Social Science Encyclopedia*, London and New York, Routledge, 2nd edn.

Landman, T. (2000) *Issues and Methods in Comparative Politics. An Introduction*, London and New York, Routledge.

Lawton, D. (1999) 'How to Succeed in Postgraduate Study', in *Working for A Doctorate: A Guide for the Humanities and Social Sciences*, London and New York, Routledge.

Lewis, P. A. (2002) 'Agency, Structure and Causality in Political Science: A Comment on Sibeon', *Politics*, 22(1), 17–23.

Lewis-Beck, M. S. (1995) *Data Analysis: An Introduction*, London, Thousand Oaks, CA and New Delhi, Sage.

Maloney, W., Smith, G. and Stoker, G. (2000) 'Social Capital and Urban Governance: Adding a More Contextualised "Top-Down" Perspective', *Political Studies*, 48, 802–20.

Marsh, D. and Furlong, P. (2002) 'A Skin, not a Sweater: Ontology and Epistemology in Political Science', in D. Marsh and G. Stoker (eds.), *Theory and Methods in Political Science* (Basingstoke, Palgrave Macmillan), updated and revised edn, pp. 17–41.

Marsh, D. and Smith, M. J. (2001) 'There is more than one way to do Political Science: On different ways to study Policy Networks', *Political Studies*, 49, 528–41.

Mason, J. (1998) *Qualitative Researching*, London, Thousand Oaks, CA and New Delhi, Sage.

May, D. (1999) 'Planning Time', in N. Graves and V. Varma (eds), *Working for a Doctorate. A Guide for the Humanities and Social Sciences*, London and New York, Routledge.

May, T. (2001) *Social Research. Issues, Methods and Process*, Buckingham, Open University Press.

McAnulla, S. (2002) 'Structure and Agency', in D. Marsh and G. Stoker (eds), *Theory and Methods in Political Science*, Basingstoke, Palgrave Macmillan, updated and revised edn.

McFalls, L. (2001) 'Constructing the New East German Man, 1961–2001, or Bringing Real Culture Back to Political Science', manuscript.

Merton, R. K. (1967) *On Theoretical Sociology*, New York, The Free Press.

Neuman, W. L. (2000) *Social Research Methods. Qualitative and Quantitative Approaches*, Boston, MA, Allyn & Bacon, 4th edn.

Outhwaite, W. (1986) *Understanding Social Life: The Method called 'Verstehen'*, London, Allen & Unwin.

Paterson, W. E. (1996). 'Beyond Semi-Sovereignty: The New Germany in the New Europe', *German Politics*, 5(2), 167–84.

Pennings, P, Keman, H. and Kleinnijenhuis, J. (1999) *Doing Research in Political Science. An Introduction to Comparative Methods and Statistics*, London, Thousand Oaks, CA and New Delhi, Sage.

Peters, G. B. (1998) *Comparative Politics. Theory and Methods*, Basingstoke, Palgrave Macmillan.

Phillips, E. M. and Pugh, D. S. (eds) (1994) *How to Get a PhD. A Handbook for Students and their Supervisors*, Buckingham and Philadelphia, PA, Open University Press.

Plato (1994) *Republic*, trans. Robin Wakefield, Oxford and New York, Oxford University Press.

Popper, K. (2000) *The Logic of Scientific Discovery*, London and New York, Routledge.

Punch, K. F. (2000a) *Introduction to Social Research. Quantitative and Qualitative Approaches*, London, Thousand Oaks, CA and New Delhi, Sage.

Punch, K. F. (2000b) *Developing Effective Research Proposals*, London, Thousand Oaks, CA and New Delhi, Sage.

Putnam, R. (1993) *Making Democracy Work. Civic Traditions in Modern Italy*, Princeton, NJ, Princeton University Press.

Putnam, R. (1996) 'The Strange Disappearance of Civic America', *The American Prospect*, 24 (Winter).

Putnam, R. (2000) *Bowling Alone: The Collapse and Revival of American Community*, New York, Simon & Schuster.

Ragin, C. C. (1994) *Constructing Social Research. The Unity and Diversity of Method*, Thousand Oaks, CA, Pine Forge Press.

Ringer, F. (1997) *Max Weber's Methodology. The Unification of the Cultural and Social Sciences*, Cambridge, MA and London, Harvard University Press.

Robins, G. S. (1995) 'Banking in a Transition Economy: East Germany After Unification', University of Oxford, PhD thesis.

Robson, C. (1995) *Real World Research, A Resource for Social Scientists and Practitioner-Researchers*, Oxford and Cambridge, MA, Blackwell, 2nd edn. 2002.

Rosamond, B. (2000) *Theories of European Integration*, Basingstoke, Palgrave Macmillan.

Rosamond, B. (2002) 'Plagiarism, Academic Norms and the Governance of the Profession', *Politics*, 22(3), 167–74.

Rose, R. (1999) 'Getting Things Done in an Antimodern Society: Social Capital Networks in Russia', in P. Dasgupta and I. Serageldin (eds), *Social Capital. A Multifaceted Perspective*, Washington, DC World Bank.

Ross, C. and Grix, J. 'Approaches to the German Democratic Republic', in J. Grix (ed.), *Approaches to the Study of Contemporary Germany: Research Methodologies in German Studies*, Birmingham, University of Birmingham Press.

Rubinstein, D. (1981) *Marx and Wittgenstein*, London, Boston and Henley, Routledge & Kegan Paul.

Rudestam, K. E. and Newton, R. R. (1992) *Surviving your Dissertation. A Comprehensive Guide to Content and Process*, London, Thousand Oaks, CA and New Delhi, Sage.

Samuelson, P. A. (1947) *Foundations of Economic Analysis*, Cambridge, MA, Harvard University Press.

Sayer, A. (2000) *Realism and Social Science*, London, Sage.

Schnell, R., Hill, P. B. and Esser, E. (1999) *Methoden der empirischen Sozialforschung*, Munich and Vienna, Oldenbourg.

Sibeon, R. (1999) 'Agency, Structure, and Social Chance as Cross-Disciplinary Concepts', *Politics* 19(3), 139–44.

Silverman, D. (2000) *Doing Qualitative Research. A Practical Handbook*, London, Thousand Oaks, CA and New Delhi, Sage.

Steiner, G. (1991) *Real Presences*, London and Boston, Faber & Faber.

Stoker, G. (1995) 'Introduction', in D. Marsh and G. Stoker (eds), *Theory and Methods in Political Science*, Basingstoke, Palgrave Macmillan.

Stolle, D. and Rochon, T. R. (1999) 'The Myth of American Exceptionalism', in J. W. van Deth, M. Maraffi, K. Newton and P. F. Whiteley (eds), *Social Capital and European Democracy*, London and New York, Routledge.

Strauss, A. and Corbin, J. (1998) 'Grounded Theory Methodology: An Overview', in N. K. Denzin and Y. S. Lincoln (eds), *Strategies of Qualitative Inquiry*, London, Thousand Oaks, CA and New Delhi, Sage.

Van Evera, S. (1997) *Guide to Methods for Students of Political Science*, Ithaca, NY and London, Cornell University Press.

Vickers, R. (1997) 'Using Archives in Political Research', in P. Burnham (ed.), *Surviving the Research Process in Politics*, London and Washington, DC, Pinter.

Walliman, N. (2001) *Your Research Project*, London, Thousand Oaks, CA and New Delhi, Sage.

Weber, M. (1949) *The Methodology of the Social Sciences*, trans. and ed. E. A. Shils and H. A. Finch, New York, Free Press.

Whiteley, P. (1999) 'The Origins of Social Capital', in J. W. van Deth, M. Maraffi, K. Newton and P. F. Whiteley (eds), *Social Capital and European Democracy*, London and New York, Routledge.

Williams, M. and May, T. (2000) *Introduction to the Philosophy of Social Research*, London and New York, Routledge.

Wisker, G. (2001) *The Postgraduate Handbook. Succeed with your MA, MPhil, EdD and PhD*, Basingstoke, Palgrave Macmillan.

Wood, M. (2003) *Making Sense of Statistics. A Non-Mathematical Approach*, Basingstoke, Palgrave Macmillan.

Woolcock, M. (1998) 'Social Capital and Economic Development: Toward a Theoretical Synthesis and Policy Framework', *Theory and Society, Renewal and Critique in Social Theory*, 27(2), 151–208.

Yin, R. K. (1994) *Case Study Research. Design and Methods*, London, Thousand Oaks and New Delhi, Sage, 2nd edn.

Index

Note: Page numbers in bold refer to definitions or explanations of important terms.